The Last Billion

Connecting The Dark Continent

Dave Welmans

DEDICATION

This book is dedicated to Africans of all races, colours and cultures throughout Africa and the world: those that reside on this Dark Continent and those that have left Africa and are living elsewhere in the world, but are still African at heart.

ACKNOWLEDGMENTS

Africa seems to be like the proverbial elephant in a dark room with everybody holding onto a piece of the animal and no two parts seemingly similar. These different viewpoints have helped shape this book.

Here I have laid forth my attempt at consolidating these ideas and in the writing have been pleased that I can see so much that points to an optimistic future for this continent.

My thanks to all those people who gave input and support during the writing of this. Special mention must be made of Dennis Lewis, author of The Combat Zone series of books, who encouraged me to attempt the project and Heather for being his backup, Rob McCallum for his superb editing and writing input, Hilde and Helga Munster for both their babysitting of my three dogs so I could work and Hilde for the translation into German and thanks also to Marion for always taxiing the kids so that I could work.

Finally, if you are reading this book, my thanks to you, the reader, for being interested enough in Africa and technology to spend your money on my work.

Dave Welmans

6

Dave Welmans

Preface

Shaka Zulu, the African Zulu king, (c. 1787 – c. 24 September 1828) was arguably one of the most formidable military minds of all time. His military genius is likened to that of Caesar and Hannibal. He left behind a nation that would influence tribes as far up the African continent as Lake Malawi. From a small tribe of less than 2000 men he built up a nation of 250 000 and an army of more than 20 000 *impi* warriors.

As is usually the case, when someone stands out so conspicuously, historians search for differentiating factors that Shaka introduced and employed to give him this competitive advantage. In Tom Peters' speak, Shaka Zulu becomes an apt metaphor for modern-day business.

Above the brutality needed to form this empire, which for Africa is a given, on the technological front, Shaka introduced a number of innovations that were unusual and unique in those times. Shaka is said to have been dissatisfied with the long throwing "assegai", and credited with introducing a new version of the weapon; the *"iklwa"*, a short stabbing spear with a long, sword-like spearhead.

Although Shaka probably did not actually invent the spear, according to scholar John Laband, he taught them to use the weapon to deadly effect. This 'new' weaponry gave them a *"terrifying advantage"* over their opponents who up until this time had only used the traditional throwing spear and avoided close-quarter combat. The original long spear was not totally removed but was used in the initial assault before getting close to the enemy, where the *'ikwla'* was used in hand-to-hand combat.

Shaka also introduced a cowhide shield instead of one made of wood. Each soldier was schooled to use the shield effectively in killing the enemy.

This was the application of new technology, while his introduction of new methods of apprenticeships for the young boys and his military strategy can be likened to new business methods. In fighting, he is credited with being the first general to employ the bullhorn approach on the battlefield to outflank and decimate the enemy.

On the business model side, Shaka implemented reforms to integrate defeated clans into the victorious Zulu tribe. Once absorbed in the Zulu tribe, seniority and promotions were on a basis of merit. This talks to the unprecedented nepotism prevalent in African states today.

The application of new technology combined with new methodologies in warmongering is equivalent to the introduction of new technology as well as new business strategy in all aspects of global business today. I like to call this combination of technology and African-specific strategy 'tech-strat'.

Just like Shaka, this introduction of new technology without his unique insight/strategy of how to deploy it would have failed dismally. A parallel can be drawn regarding Africa today. The unquestionable high level of technology available to the African continent is useless without an all-encompassing continental strategy and technology roadmap to effectively change the status quo and reduce the barriers of entry into the global economy.

Dave Welmans

Shaka's half-brothers finally poisoned him but the Zulu kingdom still continued to dominate the region and tribes in the sub-continent.

As in all things, the tendency of technology to bring sweeping change soon put pay to the Zulu nation's supremacy. Just as Shaka employed new technology and strategies for the ascendancy of the Zulu nation, the Zulu nation was undone by a newer and more deadly technology and strategy (tech-strat).

First, the Boers defeated the Zulus in 1838 when an army of 470 Boers defeated 21 000 Zulu *impi* at the battle of Blood River. The Boers brought cannons, cavalry and rifles to the fight, while the Zulus only had their cowhide shields and short *ikwla* assegais. Talk about a bringing a knife to a gunfight!

The result, after the battle was devastating: 3000 dead or injured Zulus and three slightly injured Boers - a perfect example of overwhelming tech-strat advantage.

Despite the Zulus being the knife-wielding party, it was not all one-way traffic. The Zulu *impi* also managed to inflict a decisive victory over the much better equipped British in the Anglo-Zulu war at the Battle of Isindwala in 1878.

The Zulus were armed with the *iklwa* assegai and cowhide shields, as well as a small number of rifles.

The British troops were armed with the modern Martini-Henry rifle and 7-pounder cannons

Despite this difference in weapons, with the British having a marked advantage in this aspect, the well-trained Zulus overwhelmed the British, who were not battle-hardened and were inexperienced in fighting in Africa. The Zulus won the battle and killed over 1300 British troops.

The battle was an overwhelming victory for the Zulus and prevented the first attempt of the British to invade Zululand. This battle was to be remembered for the worst defeat a British force ever suffered by an indigenous force in Africa or any of their colonies.

Again, the technology without a well thought-out African tech-strat is useless.

This book is an attempt to highlight how technology has had an impact in Africa. It is both focused on the historical, (mostly the near past), the current (2015), and the future impact of certain technologies and the underpinning of the importance of a deployment strategy or tech-strat in Africa and what you should know about it.

In short, I will give you a brief insight into the history, the culture and the incredible potential in Africa. Be prepared to understand the historical damage caused by slavery, colonisation, exploitation and the lack of a tech-strat on behalf of Africa over the last 500 years of this Dark Continent's history. In many ways Africa is still bringing its knife to a global economic gunfight.

Dave Welmans

1. Introduction

My story of Africa starts with a very small and poor African country, Malawi, The Warm Heart of Africa. For anyone lucky enough to have visited this wonderful country, and I have been lucky enough to visit it in excess of 50 times over the years, you will know the friendliness of the people but also the developmental backwardness of the country. That is the exact reason to visit, together with the opportunity to float in the stunning warm waters of Lake Malawi.

William Kamkwamba, a 14-year-old young rural village boy was one of the 60% of people in Africa without access to electricity and 50% with no running water. He had a dream about using technology to help his family survive the next drought like the one they had just been through.

He came across a picture of a windmill in a book in his primary school library and researched how to build one to pump water in order to irrigate his family's lands. Using true African ingenuity and an adaptation to his particular environment, William built a windmill to pump water for his family using mostly bicycle parts.

Taking this one step further and encouraged by his success, he added a small magneto and batteries to store this harvested energy and connected a bulb for a light inside their hut.

He would comment later that libraries like the one at his school were not that common and most schools in the area and Africa in general do not have enough books for all the students. Despite a shortage of books, William was lucky enough to have access to this library. USAID and other NGO's funded the school making it a particularly fortunate school.

William's Windmill – Ted.com

William discovered books and those that most caught his attention were the science books. A windmill driven water-pump that he saw in one of these intrigued him.

Using his own ingenuity and old bicycle parts, William built a water-pump for his family. Once complete he adapted it to drive a dynamo and run a light bulb in their hut as well as setting it up to charge cellphone batteries.

In true African fashion, the word soon spread - in part probably helped by the beacon of light in their hut - and

Dave Welmans

before long, he was the local cellphone charging station with people queuing up to make use of his creation.

This story illustrates a number of critical and fundamentally African paradigms.

- Not having electricity or water is the norm in Africa.
- Foreign aid money is still important.
- People need to travel to a physical location to find out something.
- William adapted his acquired knowledge to local conditions.
- He adapted his 'device' to add other functionality.
- He was happy to share his invention.
- The neighbours soon found out about the device through the African grapevine.
- They chose to use this technology to charge their cellphones!

In Africa we could redefine Maslow's hierarchy of needs as above.

This highlights the skewness of Maslow's hierarchy in Africa. The need for communication is paramount. Even above other expected survival amenities.

This story took place in the early 2000's. My first excursion into Africa was in 1989, when I first ventured into Deepest Darkest Africa – which happened to be a trip to Malawi, the same 'Warm heart of Africa' from the story above.

Despite growing up in South Africa, the rest of Africa was still seen as unknown by many South Africans.

The year was 1989 and it was still six years before the first cellular network was rolled out in Africa. I remember explaining to family that they should not expect much contact from me on my three-week venture at all; possibly a telegram, as I wasn't keen to spend a few hours in the overcrowded post office in Blantyre waiting for hours to make a phone call back to South Africa. I was going to the Lake anyway, where I would have had even less chance getting access to a telephone.

Comparing my first visit to Malawi to the last time I drove through the country – on a trip from South Africa to Tanzania, a trip of a mere 4000km, driving up the whole length of this beautiful lake, I noticed a radical change in the status of communications in Africa. This time, in 2013, we activated roaming or bought a local cellular number for a dollar or so and messaged people at home as to our progress. It still wasn't possible to upload pictures onto Facebook, as the networks did not support anything more than voice traffic.

Dave Welmans

What had happened in the interim was the initial roll-out of cellular communications networks throughout Africa.

Telecoms or communication becomes the basis for personal and business interaction. The change in Africa was from one of *no* communication to the almost ubiquitous and pervasive ability to contact anyone *anywhere*. (In 2015, 75% of Africans can be reached on cellphones).

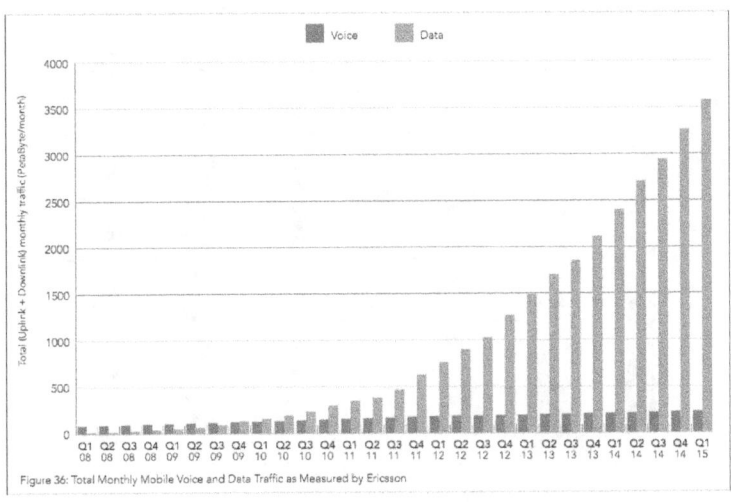

Figure 36: Total Monthly Mobile Voice and Data Traffic as Measured by Ericsson

The State of the Internet, Quarter 1, 2015 – Akamai

The telecoms revolution has already started in Africa.

This graph shows the voice and data growth of cellular networks worldwide. I fully expect Africa to follow a similar trend of moving from voice only networks to voice and data networks. In most instances, the smartphone is the only connection to the Internet and will drive the need for its adoption. It is the availability of cheap smartphones and the evolution of cellular networks to carry data that will facilitate the growth of mobile data in Africa.

The graph below shows that data revenue on mobile networks in Africa lags far behind the voice revenue trend but is following a similar growth curve as the world trend above.

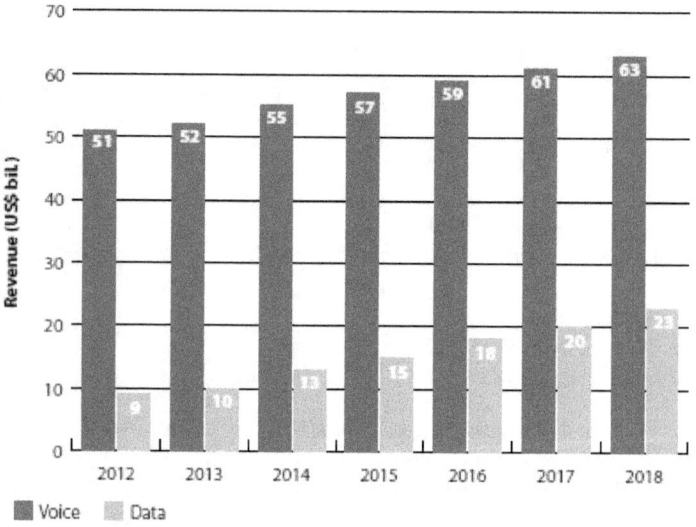

Source: Informa Telecoms & Media

Africa, mobile service revenue forecasts, 2012-2018

One of the major reasons for this lag is the late introduction of cheap smartphones in a price sensitive market and the slower upgrading of cellular networks to be able to handle data or broadband connectivity.

Dave Welmans

In the next chapter I cover the mind-blowing misconception as to the size of the African continent and the potential impact this may have on the global economy in the future.

Dave Welmans

2. Size Matters in Africa

Africa Infographic – Andile.co.za

When I was at school, I always knew I was being lied to by the powers that be. Imagine a landmass that covers 20% of the earth's world surface and is home to 15 % of the world's population. And yet we paid it scant attention besides the small corner that we happened to live in and called home. This substantial portion of the world's landmass goes under a single name: AFRICA. And yet the map that we used in school didn't depict its size with anything approaching reality.

The Mercator distortion

It is a common misconception that Africa is as seen in terms of the Mercator projection of the world. Even in the distorted

Mercator depiction it can be seen that Europe and the USA could easily fit into the continent of Africa.

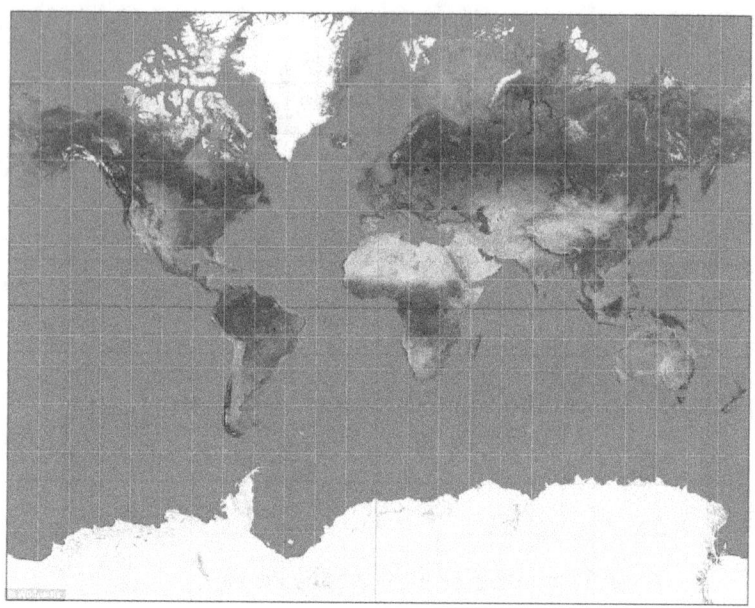

Mercator projection of world map – Wikipedia

To point out how inaccurate this widely accepted misconception is, have a look at Greenland. It appears to be about the same size as Africa. In reality Africa is 15 times the size of Greenland: 2m km^2 versus 30m km^2.

The graphic below put together by Kai Krause was the first map that drew this inaccuracy to my attention. It is earth-shaking to say the least when seen in this light.

The amazing map shows that China, United States, Britain, Spain, France, Germany, Italy, Japan, the whole of Eastern

Dave Welmans

Europe and, if that wasn't enough, the whole of India all fit comfortably into the continent of Africa. Even this mind-challenging depiction has its inaccuracies. The United Kingdom is shown as approximately the size as Madagascar – the island off the east coast of southern Africa – whereas in reality, it is only half the size of this island.

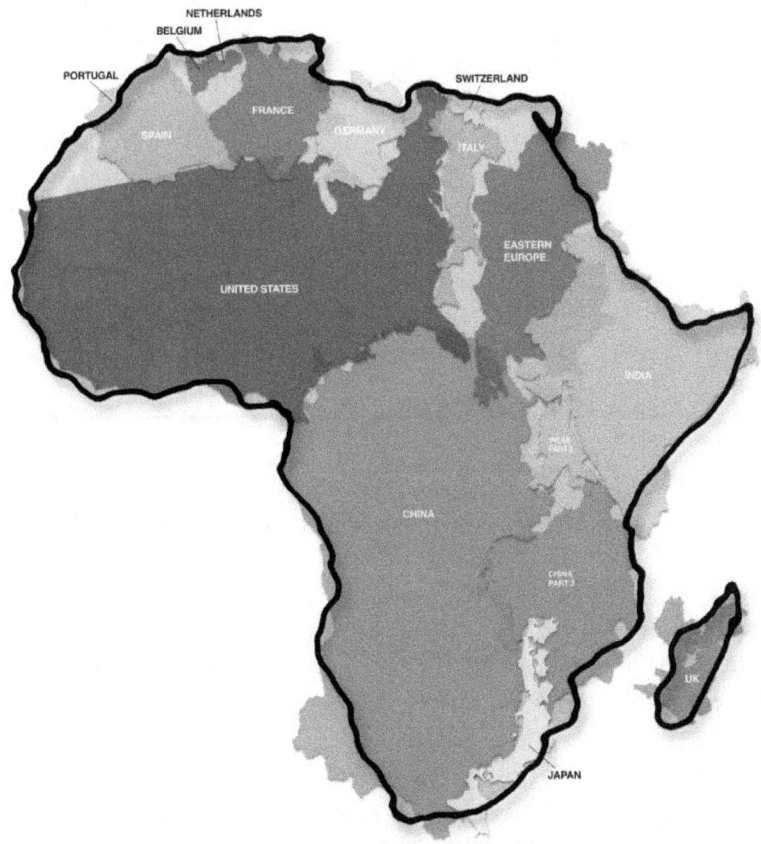

Source: http://kai.sub.blue/en/africa.html

This simple map should highlight that Africa is massively underestimated, and by almost any means of measurement, Africa is the untapped, underestimated and misunderstood Dark Continent.

The table below shows the statistics for Africa compared to other continents. Africa has as many people as China or India and more inhabitants than the whole of Europe and North America combined while also having 52 cities of >1m people.

	India	Africa	China	Europe	Latin America	North America
Population (million)	1,219	1,032	1,351	830	594	349
Cities with > 1 million people	48	52	109	52	63	48

Source: McKinsey Global Institute (2010)

Source: Visa Africa Integration Index - McKinsey Global Institute (2010)

Together these two pieces of information should further highlight the misconception that the rest of the world has about the sheer size and number of people in Africa.

The wealth map below of world Gross Domestic Product (GDP), represented by size, will give another view of Africa showing the lack of industry, commerce and development in Africa.

Dave Welmans

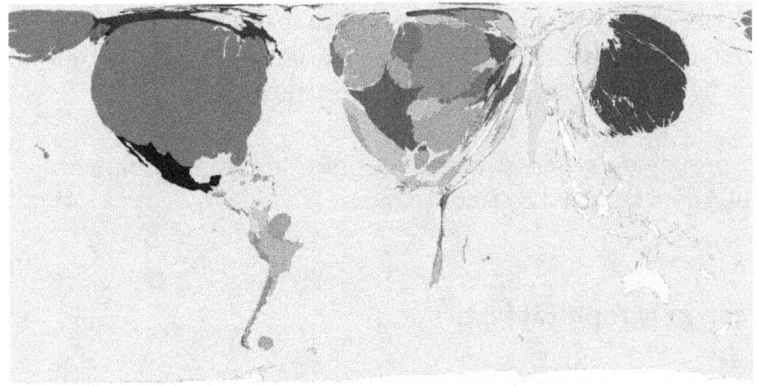

Wealth Map showing GDP - Worldmapper

It highlights the dormant nature of Africa's vast potential. Africa accounts for 2.4% of the world's GDP.

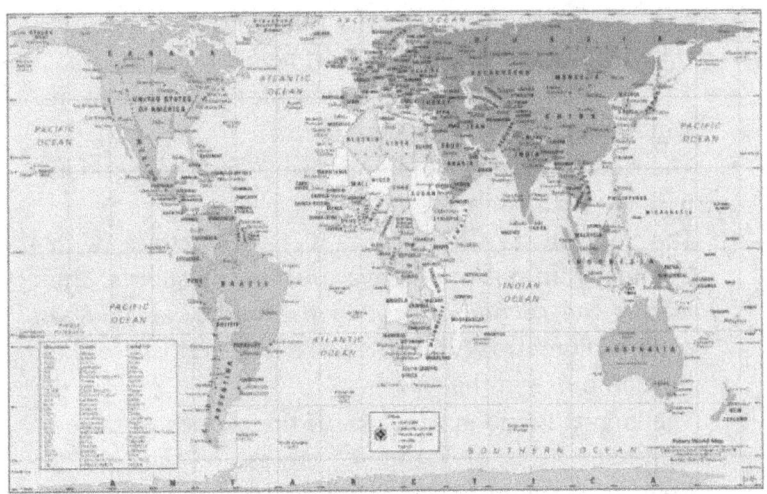

Gall-Peters world map

The Last Billion

Looking for a more realistic view of Africa led me to discover this Gall-Peters world map above, which is the best depiction I've come across. It shows the world with landmasses correctly depicted according to their relative sizes.

Map propaganda notwithstanding, here are some numbers about Africa supplied by About Travel.

African geographical facts

- There are 54 countries in Africa with South Sudan being Africa's newest country, coming into existence in 2011.
- The tallest mountain is Mount Kilimanjaro in Tanzania: 5895m / 19 340 feet. – A peak I have had the pleasure of climbing.
- The lowest point in Africa is found at Lake Assal in Djibouti at a mere 155m (515 ft) below sea level.
- The Sahara desert is the largest desert in Africa at almost 9m km^2 (3.5m square miles).
- The Nile is the longest river in Africa and the world at 6650km (4132 miles) long.
- The largest lake in Africa is Lake Victoria with Uganda, Tanzania and Kenya touching its shores. The lake is the second largest in the world, at 68 800 square kilometres (26 560 square miles). It is also the official source of the Nile.
- The largest island in Africa is off the east coast of the continent. It is also the 4th largest in the world. Madagascar is just over 1580km (1000 mi) long and 570 km (350 miles) wide. This makes it twice as large as the United Kingdom.

Dave Welmans

- Victoria Falls or *'the smoke that thunders'* is the largest waterfall in Africa. It forms part of the border between Zambia and Zimbabwe. They falls are over 1.7km wide (1mi) and 108m (355 feet) high.
- The equator runs like a belt through the middle of Africa going through Congo, Gabon, Uganda, Somalia and Kenya as well as the Democratic Republic of Congo.

Summary: Size Matters

- Africa is larger than commonly projected or understood.
- Africa is not a single homogenous state but rather 54 separate countries.
- Africa is diverse in culture, fauna and flora.
- 50% of Africans are 19 or younger.
- 50% of Africa lives below the poverty line.
- 66% of Africans have no electricity or running water.

In the next chapter of the book, I will endeavour to explain the origins of the term 'The Dark Continent' and the unsavoury connection to human slavery, the beginning of Africa's history with the First World.

This is important to lay the foundation for understanding the background of the power vacuum created by slavery and colonisation and what replaced it.

Dave Welmans

3. Africa - The Dark Continent

During the middle of the 19th century, Africa was referred to as the "Dark Continent" because little was known about the mysterious continent. The term "Dark Continent" was first used by US explorer Henry Stanley in the title of his book *"Through the Dark Continent"* published in 1878 – the same year as the defeat of the British at Isindlwana. Stanley is probably better known for his search for Livingstone in Africa with the "Dr Livingstone, I presume?" catchphrase.

European nations controlled Africa until independence in the 20th century. Despite this apparent control over hundreds of years, the interior was still unknown and not mapped out. It was only in the 19th century that a fever to explore the interior gripped the world. It was following this new discovery of Africa that led to an awareness of the abundant resources within the continent.

Africa has always been a source of wealth for those greedy enough, brutal enough and organised enough to take what they want.

The African slave trade

"Africa has always been rich. Before colonial times, Africans, Arabs, and Europeans simply took what they wanted. Slaving was a convenient way to make a maximum profit in a minimum area, a system so efficient it was imported wholesale to fuel the success of the New World."

Robert Young Pelton, 2014

The use of technologically superior forces to conquer tribes and enslave them for economic and political gains reflected a dark time on the Dark Continent.

The slave trade and how it impacted on Africa still ripples through Africa and the world economy today and lays the foundation for the African colonisation that took place over the last three centuries.

Using Africa as a source for slaves has continued for thousands of years. It was during the 17th century that the demand for cash crops such as sugar, cotton, coffee, and tobacco, which were grown in Brazil, the West Indies, and the colonies of North America, drove the demand for slave labour.

The Portuguese were the first large nationally backed slavers. The Dutch, who were in turn replaced by the French and English, supplanted them.

It is estimated that about 2 750 000 slaves were brought to the Americas during the 17th century and 7 000 000 during the 18th.

Other countries and empires have exploited Africa for centuries using their own superior technology and strategy to garnish vast wealth from Africa while leaving nothing behind. The approach of 'take it all and leave nothing' has long dominated outsiders' approach to Africa.

Dave Welmans

Colonisation – the new slavery

With the exceptions of Ethiopia and Liberia non-African countries colonised *all* of Africa.

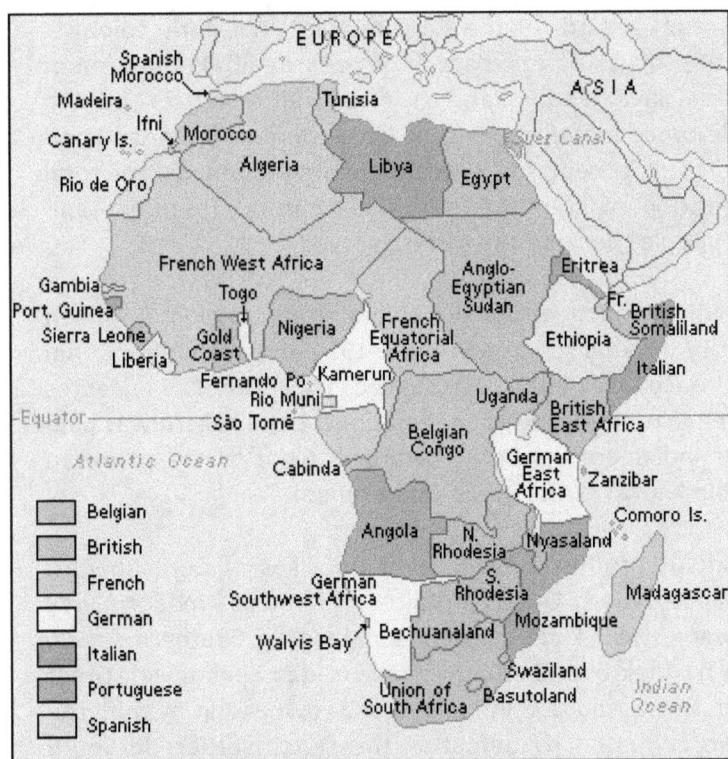

Africa after the 1884-85 Berlin Conference - Wikipedia

A whole continent whose size is immense with wealth unimaginable was appropriated by more technically advanced cultures and dished out like toys at Christmas.

The United Kingdom, France, Belgium, Spain, Italy, Germany and Portugal all claimed to rule parts of Africa without the consent of the local population.

With scant regard for the local peoples, the early colonists took the small step to create enormous wealth in the form of people (slave labour) and rich natural resources by the simple process of doing this for king, country, fatherland and Führer. This 'acceptable' process of colonisation and the total exploitation of countries and their natural resources and their peoples became the new slavery.

The rivalry among European powers for possession of African territory became so intense in the 19th century that the Berlin Conference (1884–85) was called to settle the disputes between competing European nations. Little regard was paid to the indigineous people as borders were drawn up in the sqabble known as the Berlin Conference.

Individuals profited hugely as in the likes of Cecil Rhodes, who persuaded Great Britain to annexe modern day Botswana, then know as Bechuanaland, in Southern Africa, while he took over Zambezia (current day Zimbabwe). Great Britain increased its influence and ownership within the African continent by defeating the Dutch settlers in South Africa in the Boer War of 1899–1902. This also led to the annexing of the gold rich provinces of the Transvaal and the Orange Free State. This illustrates how 'normal' it was for war to be used to extend an individual's and an empire's wealth and land.

With few exceptions, colonisation was as brutal as the slave trade. This imperialism was only a thin veneer of politics and

Dave Welmans

nationalism to cover individuals' enormous greed. Eventually, after the First World War and over the following decades and after a century of exploitation, European countries began to feel the need to replace colonisation with something more equitable and less troublesome.

The huge human cost of World War II left countries with little appetite to continue their own brutal practices. The feeling after World War II and expressed in MacMillan's "Winds of Change" speech in the British parliament in 1963 led to an acceleration of African countries gaining independence.

Independence movements

These European colonial powers changed their imperialist approach to one more concerned with independence of the former colonies and matters like education and social freedom. From the colonies' viewpoint, a burgeoning nationalistic passion engulfed Africa with demands for independence.

From the 50's onwards, former colonies attained independence. Sudan in 1956 and Ghana in 1957 were some of the first to attain independence from Britain. In 1958 Guinea became independent from France. The rush to independence reached its height in the 60's and 70's with 17 nations gaining independence. The few remaining countries followed in the next decades.

The new African nations

Newly independent nations barely survived with coups and assassinations being the order of the day in the first 30 years of independence.

As will happen when a vacuum is created, caused by the withdrawal of the ruling imperialists, it was filled with so-called legitimate governments. I use the term 'so-called' because in most cases the only difference between legitimate and those deemed as not legitimate, was the recognition of their nationhood by the original European colonial power. The 80's saw an Africa with former colonial borders inherited by these fragile governments. These borders that remained were created by the Berlin Conference and had little to do with defined African populations. With this withdrawal of colonial oversight, not surprisingly, many African governments fell to coups and soon became dictatorships or were governed by military rule in the years that followed.

Many African countries were torn by devastating civil wars in the following decades. Countries in which civil wars were fought - in some cases for more than a decade - include Angola, Namibia, Chad, Mozambique, Nigeria, Sudan, Uganda, and the Democratic Republic of the Congo. Despite the fighting, most of the colonial-era borders remain as defined at the Berlin Conference a century before.

Of interest to us is one of the bloodiest such conflicts occurring in Rwanda and Burundi in 1994. On the surface, it seemed that this war was all about ethnic hatred and the

Dave Welmans

intense conflict resulted in the genocide of more than 700 000 people over a period of a few months.

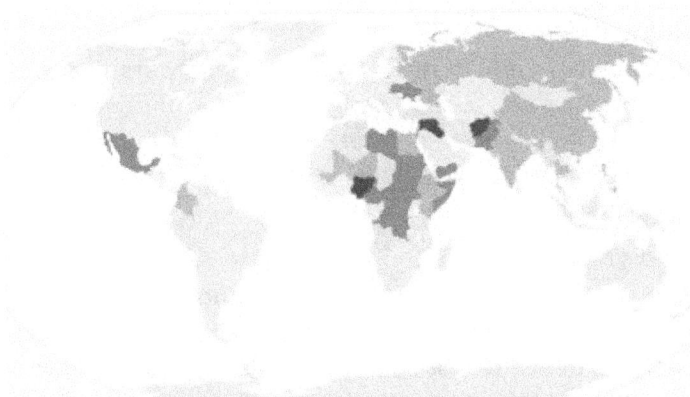

Locations of on-going conflicts worldwide, February 2015
▌Major wars, 10,000+ deaths in current or past year
▌Wars, 1000–9999 deaths in current or past year
▌Minor conflicts, 100-999 deaths in current or past year
▐ Skirmishes and clashes, fewer than 100 deaths in current or past year: **Wikipedia**

The 1960's black liberation movements spread across Africa against still white-dominated governments. These liberation wars were often brutal and long lasting. In 1975 Mozambique and Angola finally gained their independence; Rhodesia, now Zimbabwe, became independent in 1980 and in 1990 South West Africa became Namibia. South Africa was the last such country to shrug off white-dominated rule in 1994.

The enormous wealth in Africa still lends itself to exploitation by the most brutal and it is only with the dawning of connectedness in the form of the Internet that the outside world now sees some of these practices that have been taking place for time immemorial.

Technology and war

In 2015, Africa is home to most of the current wars in the world as shown by the conflict map above. It is the world's insatiable need for Africa's natural resources that drives a large portion of these conflicts.

The unknown war

As already mentioned concerning the Rwandan Genocide above, this 'ethnic' war continued almost unabated across its neighbours' borders proving that economics are the major driver of this conflict and ethnic hatred is merely the convenient rationale adopted in the western press. The Second Congo War has claimed more than 5.4m lives in the Eastern DRC between 1998 and 2003 and still continues today. The figure of 5.4m deaths is almost as many as those incurred in the Vietnam conflict and yet it still remains a relatively unknown and under-reported conflict.

The Second Congo War is the deadliest war in modern African history; it has involved nine African countries, as well as about 20 armed groups. By 2008, the war and its aftermath had killed 5.4m people, making the Second Congo War the deadliest conflict worldwide since World War II.

What shocks most people is the brutality exhibited by Africans on Africans. Joseph Kony and his Lords' Resistance Army (LRA) are but one example. Abduction of children for

Dave Welmans

the use as child warriors, and almost unthinkable brutality in maintaining this control – including the amputation of limbs as a means of punishment – continue to shock the world and yet these brutal tortures were inherited from Africa's colonial masters over the previous centuries of subjugation.

Despite these horrific numbers, most of the rest of the world is unaware of these enormously devastating conflicts even though Joseph Kony of the Lord's Resistance Army became a YouTube phenomenon with over 100m views with the "Kony 2012" video. Despite this infamy, Kony is still at large today, although no one quite knows what happened to him, showing that Africa is big enough for a 2000-person army to disappear.

This on-going conflict has DRC's government forces backed by Angola, Namibia and Zimbabwe struggling for control against rebels backed by Uganda and Rwanda.

Rare earth metals

Greed drives conflict and the Congo conflict has an economic and a political side. Fighting is fuelled by the country's vast mineral wealth, with all sides taking advantage of the anarchy to plunder natural resources. Unluckily, for now, this part of the world has an inordinate amount of 'rare earth metals'.

Rare earth metals are a series of chemical elements found in abundance in this part of Africa and not in any meaningful quantity anywhere else except China. These metals have particular characteristics that make them vital to many modern electronic devices.

The irony is that the telecoms revolution happening in Africa is also the economic catalyst for this conflict over rare earth metals.

Cassiterite, coltan, and wolframite are the three main minerals that are sought after. They are often referred to as the 3T minerals as they are used to derive tin, tantalum, and tungsten.

New legislation today requires companies to check and declare which mines or smelters the materials used are sourced from in Africa in an effort to reduce the outlet for these minerals.

The problem is that there are not enough conflict-free classified smelters to supply the demand from the electronics giants and so the price remains high for these minerals and the conflict continues.

The legacy of war

The after-effects of these wars are felt not only in the political instability and economic desolation but also in very real and dangerous unrecovered ordinance, mostly in the form of landmines. It is livestock and the surrounding inhabitants that deal with this every day.

A legacy from these wars is unrecovered landmines: 10-20m in Angola, 3m in Mozambique.

Dave Welmans

Tank as playground – Angola.

Summary: The Dark Continent

- Africa has survived both slavery and colonisation.
- All of Africa was colonised by non-African countries.
- From 1998-2003 5.4m people died as a result of the Second Congo War.
- There is a strong correlation between this conflict and the world's need for rare earth metals in, amongst other things, the smartphone.
- The irony is that the smartphone may be Africa's greatest liberator.
- War has left many African countries with a legacy of landmines and minefields.

Leaving the landmines behind, in the next section I will delve into what the current economic situation is and how it has changed fundamentally over the last 15 years and what this could mean to doing business in Africa.

Dave Welmans

4. Economics and finance

The Third World

Third World? What happened to the Second World? The First World is not defined as any industrialised or developed country but more accurately a developed capitalist country of Western ideology.

Third World was a cold-war naming convention to identify those former colonies that the Russians and Americans were vying for influence over. The Soviets were, in fact, the Second World.

Having survived colonisation, Africa's newly independent countries found themselves battling for economic support from the two super powers in the 70's. Despite some ties to their former colonial overlords, many countries continued to struggle to exist independently. The countries in Africa were left unprepared for the task of nation building leading to a continent of 'weak states' that were seen by the rest of the world as developing nations.

Today the term generally denotes countries that have not developed to the same levels as Organisation for Economic Co-operation and Development (OECD) countries, and are thus in the process of developing.

Economist Peter Bauer studied these economies and found that another way to define these countries is that they all demand and receive western aid. This is not surprising given their history and inability of most countries to survive and grow their economies.

"A third view of the 'Third World' is that they are normally in the southern hemisphere, were former colonies, have fast growing populations that are becoming urbanised and are still dependent on foreign aid."

The truths and fictions of the Africa rising story - Satter

The history as outlined for Africa over the last few centuries including the 20th seems to be one of no hope for Africa and when we look at the growth rate during the 1900's for Africa against the rest of the world, this seems to be borne out.

Interestingly enough, the slower growth experienced by Africa coincides with the era of colonial rule in Africa.

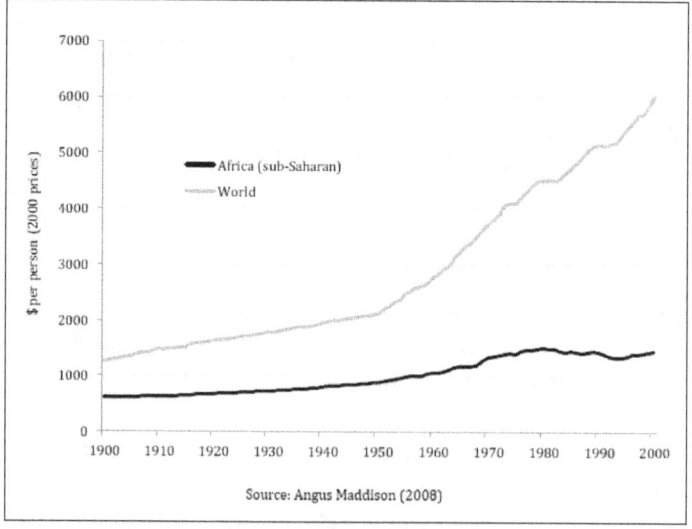

Source: Angus Maddison (2008)

Income per person 1900-2000.

Dave Welmans

But, the new millennium has brought about a change in outlook for Africa. Sattar writes a brilliant article into economic insights for Africa called *"The truths and fictions of the Africa rising story"*.

"The truth about Africa rising is that it is real. The economy is growing and potential for huge and sustained growth is enormous."

The truths and fictions of the Africa rising story - Satter

He notes that 31m households in Africa have moved out of poverty into a new consumer class. Africa will also have the largest labour force in the world within 20 years. Satter believes that this new demographic and their spending power will help fuel the African economy.

Straus and Leonard in *"Africa's stalled development"* identify possible causes and cures for current African economic issues. The causes are mostly historical in nature but are perpetuated by what they term 'weak states', foreign aid and enclave industries. The enclave industry is one that is easy to control and exact an income due to its localised nature.

The reality is that Africa is still predominantly reliant on primary industries such as mining, agriculture, or forestry, that are concerned with obtaining or providing natural raw materials for conversion into commodities and products for the First World consumer.

There is very little secondary and tertiary beneficiation industry in Africa that takes advantage of Africa's own raw materials.

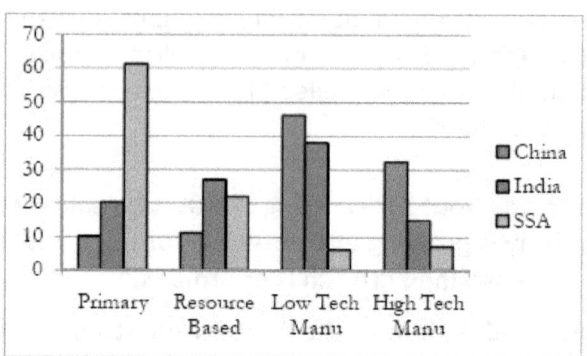

Figure 1: Comparative Export Structures, 1995
Source: Kaplinsky and Morris, 2007, table 5.

Source - Visa Sub-Saharan Integration report

As an example, Nigeria is one of the largest oil producers in the world yet all this industry exists to extract the raw product and pass it on to another country to refine. There still remains very little refining capacity in Nigeria.

The former colonists and their multi-national companies want to keep Africa as a primary provider in the global market supply chain and not build countries that can compete with finished high-tech goods. They already have China to compete with.

This is an example of other countries using their tech-strat to keep the rich African continent as indentured slaves and suppliers of much needed commodities to the world market. At best, Africa might be seen as a growing market for their own goods. But the last 15 years have seen a moving away from direct exploitation towards a more engaging and inclusive approach that has at its core the beneficiation of Africans as a whole.

Dave Welmans

Africa still needs to grow into the other areas of productivity if it is to become meaningfully integrated into the world economy and not swop colonisation for a form of economic imperialism.

The African story has changed dramatically over the past 15 years.

Africa has come a long way. It is now 70 years since independence for some countries and many of these countries are establishing stable democratic governments. These countries show stable legal systems and respect for individual property rights with efficient tax systems and much better long-term economic outlooks. All these are prerequisites to attract more direct foreign investment. The future for Africa is better than at any other time in history.

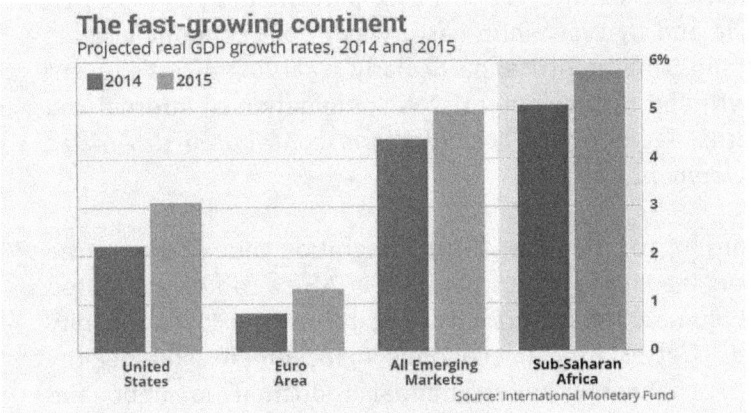

GDP 2014-2015, IMF

Writing about Nigeria and Africa for *The Wall Street Journal*, Ian Birrell says:

"There is nothing illusory about the rapid growth and rampant change across the continent. Profound problems remain, as in other parts of the world - but much of Africa stands on the brink of take-off comparable to China's. Those who fail to see this are likely to regret their anachronistic attitude."

The last 15 years has caused previous naysayers to rethink their views on Africa. Even *The Economist* retracted its famous statement in December 2000 that Africa was the *"Hopeless Continent"* in December 2011 by proclaiming *"Africa Rising"* and, more recently in March 2013, featured the cover story "Aspiring Africa", with a special report on *"Emerging Africa"*.

The Visa Africa Integration Index presented by Prof Adrian Saville and Dr Lyal White has a wealth of economic insights into sub-Saharan Africa, particularly regarding Africa's recent growth and further potential. A combination of internal and external factors have *"colluded and contributed to Africa's development."*

According to The Visa Africa integration index reports the factors leading to the turnaround in Africa can be attributed to a number of factors including robust world commodity prices, better African economic management and healthy policy changes. The substantial reduction in debt and increase in international trade has led to private investment and an increase in capital flows into Africa. All these factors have made a contribution to Africa's positive trajectory.

Dave Welmans

"Currently, whilst Africa may be the world's fastest growing continent, it also is the world's least globalised – or internationally integrated – region."

The Visa's Africa Integration Index, Saville & White

Although this seems like bad news on the face of it, it does also mean that the greatest immediate benefit, which is substantial, can be achieved by focussing on local integration in Africa, which they identify as the easiest way to unlock some of Africa's potential. That's good news!

The framework presented by Saville and White describes the nature and influence of globalisation as a key driver of material improvements in a country's economic and social welfare. Yet, in the case of African economies this element of economic integration has largely been ignored.

The growth over the 15 years also coincides with the introduction of cellular technology and it is this technology together with all the economic fundamentals explored by Saville and White that is helping to unlock the potential within Africa.

The telecoms revolution will help integrate Africa into the world economy and allow Africans access to these world markets.

The Last Billion has as its main focus the Sub-Saharan region but does give some attention to the northern African countries. Notably their culture and the basis of their economies are different to the rest of Africa. The northern African countries are oil-based economies with a strong Arab culture and influence that sets them apart somewhat from our generalised view of Africa and Africans.

African Debt

Saville and White report that in Africa in the mid-1990s, 21 out of 48 countries had debt-to-GDP ratios of >90%. ... Africa's economies faced a "debt trap."

The Visa's Africa Integration Index, Saville & White

Africa's debt-to-GDP ratio in the mid-1990s stood at 66.7%. By 1995, almost half of Africa's economies faced "debt traps". Moreover, 10 out of the measured 48 countries showed debt-to-GDP ratios above 150% in 1995.

This situation of very high debt that Africa displayed in the 1990s has changed fundamentally over the past decade. By 2010, the average debt-to-GDP ratio had halved from its 1995 level to 32.6%. The number of African countries with ratios in excess of 90% had fallen from 10 to 3. This debt reduction has numerous benefits, including lower interest on other loans. In turn, this healthier financial state translates into higher economic growth.

The strategy to reduce this debt was the implementation of massive debt reduction packages under the Heavily Indebted Poor Countries (HIPC) program that was initiated by the IMF and the World Bank.

Since the programme was initiated in 1996 it has provided debt relief and low interest rate loans to cancel or reduce external debt repayments to sustainable levels amongst poor, heavily indebted countries.

Dave Welmans

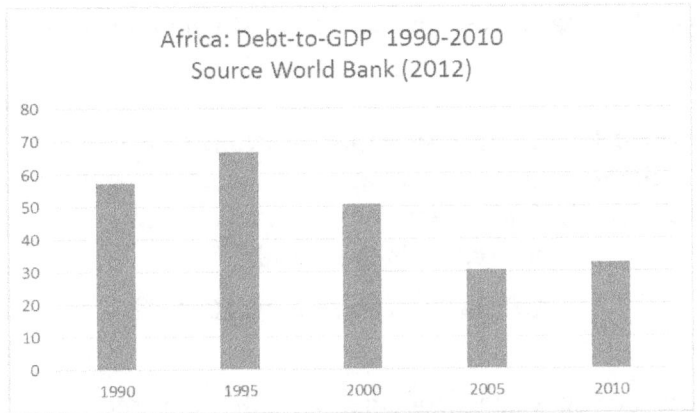

The Visa's Africa Integration Index

The improvement in debt-to-GDP ratios outlined above shows the success of this programme, which has hinged on the benefits of a reduced debt burden giving many economies a leg up onto the ladder of socio-economic advance, as opposed to the debilitating grind of debt servicing. Given the positive impact that this single initiative of debt reduction has had on Africa, it would be logical to further promote some form of debt reduction or cancellation. Jubilee 2000 is a program in this vein that also advocates debt reduction for poor countries.

"Things have changed for the better in Africa and it is expected that this aspect of buoyant economic growth will continue for the foreseeable future"

The Visa's Africa Integration Index

In 2014 Africa has a gross domestic product (GDP) of over $1.9 trillion – and this is expected to reach $2.6 trillion by

2020 – making Africa one of the world's fastest growing regions, which translates into exciting investment prospects.

> **"Whilst Africa's economic fate for a long time was associated with a reliance on foreign aid, the region now boasts the highest rate of return on investment of any region in the world."**
> **The African Progress Report, 2014**

This is what is changing: together with the debt reduction and improvement in economic fundamentals, the advent of cellular phone technology is proving to be immensely useful, over and above the basic function of communication. This in itself has contributed to an improved business environment, as cellular technology can be used for the gathering and redistributing of information, all of which help in the integration of economies. There are huge opportunities for entrepreneurs to develop cellphone applications, or apps, for specific African situations so that more information can be collected and shared, which will lead to better decision-making.

> **"The long-term solution is universal primary and secondary education. The immediate and short-term solution is to use technology to fill in the data gaps. Computers can process and relay masses of data, but are not accessible to the rural and urban poor populations."**
> **The truths and fictions of the Africa rising story - Satter**

Dave Welmans

The use of this now ubiquitous technology is paramount to help educate and inform previously isolated communities. The introduction of this single technology provides the first wave of the greatest opportunity that Africa has ever seen.

The wealth of Africa

MAPPING AFRICA'S NATURAL RESOURCE WEALTH: SELECTED COUNTRIES AND COMMODITIES

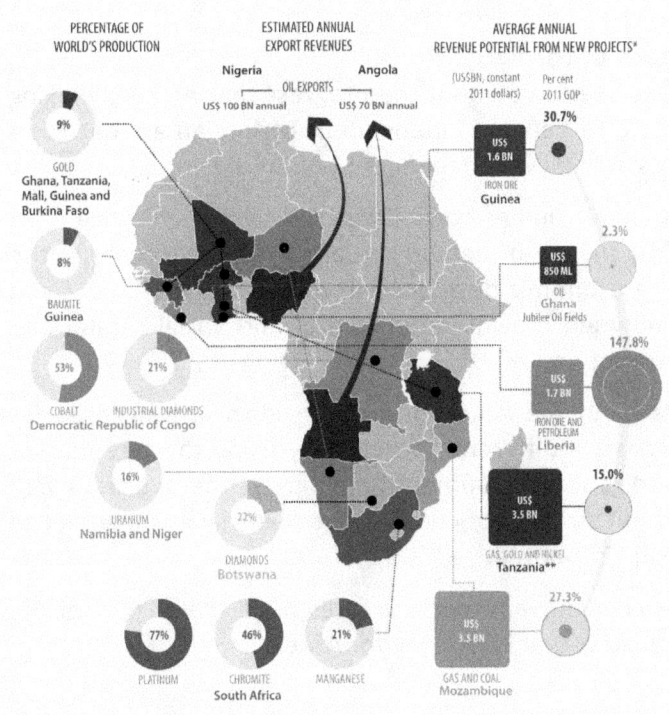

Sources: Raw Materials Data, IntierraRMG, 2013
World Bank, Africa Pulse October 2012, Volume 6
IMF, Fiscal Regimes for Extractive Industries: Design and Implementation, 2012
U.S. Geological Survey, Mineral commodity summaries 2013
*Estimates are intended to show order of magnitude. Revenue projections are highly sensitive
to assumptions about prices, phasing of production, and underlying
production and capital costs
**Data represents annual revenue at peak production

www.africaprogresspanel.org **AFRICA PROGRESS PANEL**

The African Progress Panel, 2013

Africa is the richest continent in the world when it comes to raw materials and resources. The map above gives a brilliant view of some of the potential that resides within the continent: 77% of the world's platinum, 53% of the cobalt. The right hand side of the infographic shows the possible projects as a percentage of that country's GDP, which serves to highlight the untapped potential of Africa.

The death of foreign aid
Much has been said about the progress that Africa is making as a whole to become independent of foreign aid but most countries are still very dependent on this aid.

Dambisa Moya, in her book *"Dead Aid"*, argues that we need to destroy the myth that aid actually works. She analyses the history of economic development over the last 50 years and shows how aid crowds out financial and social capital and feeds corruption.

Moyo lays out the failure of foreign aid to African countries and suggests a different approach by using the free-market system to raise development funding. In other words, a well thought out strategy of constructive financial engagement to replace aid is mooted.

It is this changing approach to foreign aid that is part of the new tech-strat that is working for Africa.

China colonises Africa
China has awoken to the returns that are available in Africa. Possibly driven by their thirst for natural resources to fuel their economy and a higher threshold for risk-taking, has led

China to engage with Africa and become their biggest trading partner. At the same time, this engagement strategy allows China to make Africa an export market for their goods.

The growth of the Chinese economy has helped Africa. Starting from a negligible base, China now trades more than $200bn worth of goods in 2013 according to The Economist.

Unfortunately, most of this trade is made up of exports of raw materials to China.

Although this appears to be one-way trade, China is also focussing on Africa as a market for its goods.

The nature of these exports from China is also changing from one of light industrial products to more technological goods. Cellphones, computers and telecoms equipment manufacturers are focussing on Africa for their goods.

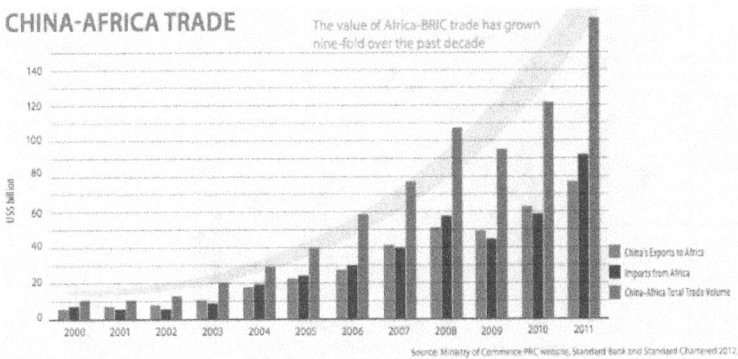

CHINA-AFRICA TRADE

As the economies of Africa grow, China will already have a foothold on the continent for its manufactured goods.

Huawei, a Chinese telecoms manufacturer, is already well entrenched in Africa and has opened up offices on the continent.

Chinese companies are also focusing on investments in Africa. Titus Mbuya, managing director of the MMEGI newspaper in Botswana, says:

"We'd love to have more Chinese investments, because African countries need to create jobs for their people. If China brings investments, establishes companies in African countries, jobs will be created. China has never colonised Africa."

This quote bears out the deep wound that still exists in Africa regarding slavery and colonisation.

China's top five trading partners in Africa
Trade value in US$ (2010)

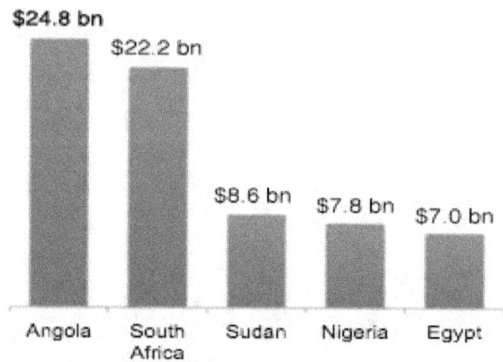

Source: China Customs, Frontier Advisory Analysis

Perhaps it is time for the rest of the world to learn from China in this regard.

Dave Welmans

Corruption Index

Here's a world map of the 2014 Corruption Perceptions Index by Transparency International. Africa features strongly on the corruption front.

The majority of African countries are listed as having endemic corruption. Strauss and Leonard identify this as one of the biggest hurdles holding back Africa.

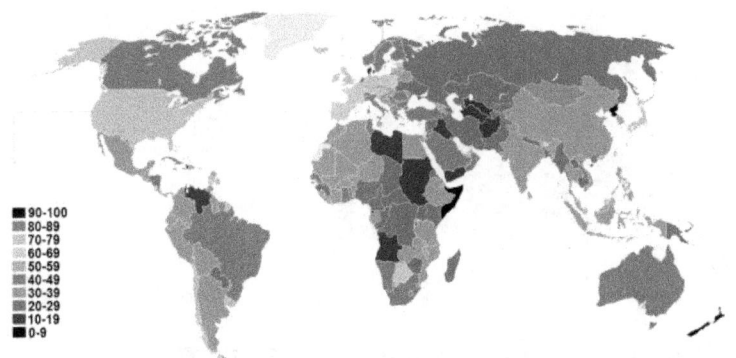

90-100
80-89
70-79
60-69
50-59
40-49
30-39
20-29
10-19
0-9

Transparency International 2014

They examine what allows a country to become corrupt and conclude that the ability of African presidents to use their state office as personal vehicles for wealth contaminates the rest of the economy. This is the major factor inhibiting the transformation of economic growth into sustained growth that delivers benefits to its citizens.

It is my fervent hope that the increasing digitisation and connectivity of the continent helps curb this constraint on Africa's growth.

Summary: Economics and Finance

Independence has brought with it its own set of problems but, finally, in the 21st century, economic and political progress is being made. The last 15 years have seen a strong upswing in progress and potential – a time that also coincides with the introduction of the cellphone.

FIGURE 25 FROM PEAK TO PLATEAU: AID FLOWS ARE FALLING AS A SHARE OF AFRICA'S GDP

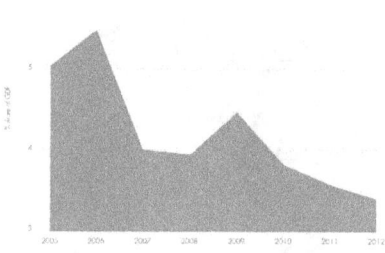

Aid flows as a percentage of national GDP. **The Visa's Africa Integration Index, Saville & White**

- The Third World is a term coined during the Cold War of the Seventies.
- Africa has shown the highest economic growth in the world over the last 10 years.
- The African economy is growing and potential for huge and sustained growth is enormous.
- Despite this growth, Africa is the world's least integrated region.
- The HIPS program has helped African countries reduce their debt-GDP ratios over the last 20 years.

Dave Welmans

- Foreign aid crowds out other traditional forms of funding.
- China is Africa's largest trading partner.
- Africa scores low on the World Corruption Index.

The next chapter deals with a starving Africa and how technology can change this.

Dave Welmans

5. The begging bowl of Africa

Despite the good news on economics in Africa in the previous chapter, Africa still has a long way to go. The world's perception of Africa as being unable to sustain itself and needing food aid just to avoid millions of people dying from starvation is a persevering one and often is not far from the truth.

"Africa's resources should be sustainably managed for the benefit of Africa's peoples. The international community must develop multilateral systems that prevent the plunder of Africa's resources."

The APP report, 2014

As laid out in the previous chapter, Africa may be showing impressive growth, but this improvement has not filtered down to the average African. To transform Africa needs to significantly increase its agriculture and fisheries sectors as these provide livelihoods for two thirds of all Africans.

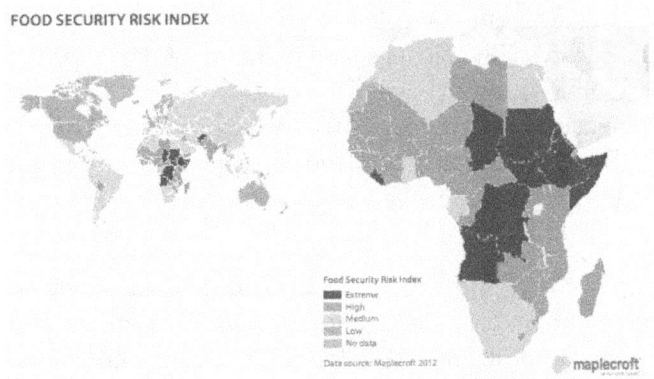

FOOD SECURITY RISK INDEX

World food scarcity map – Maplecroft

The images that Sir Bob Geldof made famous in the Eighties with his Band Aid concert that raised $150m for the crisis in Ethiopia still persist. Many argue that the slowness of the delivery of this aid and the rampant corruption and diversion of food highlighted all that is wrong in Africa.

The African Progress Panel notes that Africa's food productivity could easily double within the next 5 years.

"So why are they not yet thriving? The unacceptable reality is that too many African farmers still use methods handed from generation to generation, working their lands or grazing their animals much as their ancestors have done for millennia."

Kofi Annan – The APP report, 2014

Much has been done to avert future similar crises created by droughts by providing education and infrastructure to try and prevent this recurrence, yet Africa remains the continent most at risk for food insecurity.

Africa is a continent rich in resources. Some of those resources – especially oil, gas and minerals – have driven rapid economic growth over the past decade. Yet the ultimate measure of progress is the wellbeing of its citizens and this growth has not translated into poverty or hunger reduction nor helped improve health and education for most Africans.

Most Africans live and work in rural areas principally as subsistence and small-scale farmers. It is these farmers that must be included in the development and technological revolution that is coming to Africa.

Dave Welmans

Farmers in Africa are still at risk of drought and given the effects of global warming and climate change, more so now than in the past. Despite many African governments pledging to allocate 10% of their GDP to improving and protecting agriculture in Africa, most governments have not lived up to these promises leaving farmers in the agrarian age when it comes to farming.

Operating with no fertiliser, pesticide or irrigation on fragile soils in rain-fed areas, usually with little more than a hoe, they have suffered from a combination of neglect and disastrously misplaced development strategies.

The APP report, 2014

African farmers suffer from a lack of infrastructure, financial systems to help them, and access to markets for their produce.

Basic irrigation, mechanisation, automation and education are needed to bring the African farmer into the 21st century.

A lack of decent roads prevents farmers from getting their produce to markets. Further trade barriers also prevent the African farmer from competing effectively on a global market.

Fishing and farming

Despite these setbacks, the African Progress Panel report of 2014 – with Sir Bob Geldof as a panel member - focuses on food production under the titles of 'The Green and Blue Revolutions' underpinning the potential of Africa's agriculture and fisheries.

The single most pressing challenge facing Africa's governments is to harness the continent's increasing wealth and use it to improve people's lives. Agriculture is at the heart of that challenge.

The APP report, 2014

The opportunity for growth is encouraging but comes with lots of caveats and pitfalls that need to be avoided - problems that need to be rectified for this huge potential to be realised. The APP report notes that illicit financial flows, often connected to tax evasion in the extractives industry, but also prominent in most other areas too, cost the African continent more than it receives in either international aid or foreign investment.

Here is an example of the current tech-strat not working to control this aspect yet. A new approach is needed here. Technical and financial help to African governments is now being aimed at helping reduce these illicit flows of money out of Africa.

The advent of the cellphone and mobile networks is helping change farming in Africa. Applications that deliver information on market pricing, weather and other important information can change productivity in this sector.

Farmers need access to finance to access credit and store savings as well as insurance to mitigate the risks of drought. Finance is also needed for purchase of fertilisers and pesticides. All these are necessary to help transform the subsistence farmer into a small-scale farmer.

Dave Welmans

Selling off Africa

African countries and their inhabitants are poorer than their First World counterparts both on a national and personal level. In property ownership this means that foreigners can purchase a spot in paradise (if that's in Africa) for a modest sum compared to their homelands. The local inhabitants, in effect, compete on a global open market for this property.

Despite this restriction, some countries have balanced this with a land give-away or investment program. The programs typically involve 'free' land for foreign entities willing to invest and help set up businesses in those countries.

An example of this is an Italian company that was looking to set up a forestry industry in Mozambique and were awarded 150 000 ha of fertile land in the north-east Nampula province on a 99-year lease basis. This has led to over 5m new trees being planted in 2014!

The lesson here is that there are innumerable opportunities for companies to explore and benefit fairly out of Africa. All they need to bring is their much-needed skills and some capital while Africans will supply the willing labour and natural resources as their part of the trade - a good example of a win-win application of new tech-strat methodology.

Using technology to prevent illegal fishing

The African Progress Panel report lays out the difficulties faced by African countries, as outsiders are attracted to African waters for their own fishing needs. They report that fleets from Europe remain the primary culprits but are increasingly fleets from China and other East Asian countries are fishing African waters. Greenpeace report that the majority of illegal fishing in and around Africa can be traced to vessels from East Asia and Russia.

This is a double whammy for the local African fisherman. Not only does he battle the elements with scant hep from technology, but he now faces depleted sources of fish that helps make up a substantial portion of nutrition for their communities. It is up to the international community to help control and enforce legal fishing rights around Africa.

The APP report recommends that governments ratify and implement the 2009 Port State Measures Agreement to help tackle illegal unreported and unregulated (IUU) fishing. They recommend establishing a global fishing register and increasing fines on illegal fishing.

Despite these challenges, fishing in Africa has been growing - from a base of 55 690 tonnes in 2000 to almost 600 000 tonnes in 2010. A number of African countries are contributing to this growth: Ghana, Kenya, Namibia, Nigeria and Uganda.

Fishing in Africa would fall into the definition of an enclave industry according to Strauss and Leonard. Much of the industry is corrupt and the proceeds are used to enrich local elites and multi-national companies.

On the west cost of Africa, Senegal's waters provide jobs as well as food and income for the locals. Unfortunately they also attract foreign illegal fishing fleets.

The locals have come up with an innovative way of dealing with this illegal fishing problem. The simple answer that they have implemented is to film and then report these trawlers.

Dave Welmans

The evidence is collected and handed to over to their local authorities who follow the diplomatic route to lodge complaints with the EU and other relevant bodies.

The results of these measures have resulted in a number of fines being collected and a drop in these activities in that part of Africa. The low-cost technological solution has helped in the battle against food scarcity in Africa.

The Green Revolution

African farming has long been neglected by the technological innovations that are transforming agriculture elsewhere.

The Gates Foundation and the Rockefeller Foundation have created an organisation to address this. The Alliance for a Green Revolution in Africa (AGRA) is the answer. It was set up in 2006 and operates in 17 countries in Sub-Saharan Africa. It focuses on both the spreading of information and education to help farmers as well as finance to help address some of the problems facing farmers.

The results are impressive with more than 330 new crop varieties being released to help farmers. Education and new ways to use fertilisers have increased productivity of small-scale farming. The organisation has trained more than 1m farmers in ways to improve food storage and reduce crop losses.

The finance provided is aimed at improving access to affordable credit for farmers as well as focussing on helping farmers negotiate better prices for their produce.

Poaching

In keeping with the ugly history of Africa's colonisation and liberation, the continent suffers under the weight of exploitation of its resources. A particularly ugly aspect is the world of poaching.

Fuelled mostly by the insatiable demand from the East for Africa's wildlife, there is an enormous illegal trade in Africa's animals.

Populations of wild animals, especially lions, elephants and rhinos are declining. These populations are also negatively affected by a shrinking habitat as well as on-going conflict in some countries. The illegal issuing of licenses to foreigners willing to pay high fees contributes to this problem.

Rhino horns and elephant tusks are the targets of poachers hunting for the East Asian market. This continued demand for exotic African animals is driving Africa into the equivalent of a mass extinction.

1215 rhinos were poached in South Africa alone in 2014 and there are still elephant losses due to poaching in Tanzania, Mozambique, Cameroon and other countries.

The lack of regional integration again prevents effective cross-border management. The application of better monitoring, management and prevention strategies making use of technology to protect the fauna and capture the poachers is critical for this invaluable African resource.

Summary: The begging bowl of Africa
- Africa still suffers a high risk of food scarcity.
- Farming in Africa is very out-dated and can benefit from the use of technology.

Dave Welmans

- Basic technology in the form of irrigation schemes, mechanisation, automation and access to finance and education are paramount in order to change this.
- Technology can help monitor and prevent illegal fishing, logging and poaching activities.

The next chapter will delve into the challenges of travelling in Africa.

Dave Welmans

6. Foreigners and Travelling in Africa

"Technically, on a map, Africa is 54 seething nations chock-full of white, black, brown, and yellow people of every religion and persuasion, all communicating in real time via Internet-wired coffee shops, mystical auras, largely indecipherable tribal bickering, machetes, and bullets. It's also complex, vast, and rapidly changing. But if we're really honest, at the end of the day, to many of us its just 'Africa'."

Robert Young Pelton, 2014

Non-Africans in Africa

The term 'African' has become a race descriptor and gets confused with regional identity. What do you call someone that is ethnically not of African origin but whose ancestors came to the continent over 300 years ago?

There are millions of 'non-Africans' in Africa – Anglo-Africans, Asian-Africans and Indian-Africans. Or is that African-Indians? The European colonisers left settlers and offspring covering the whole of the continent, while other immigrants flooded in from India, China and other areas, leaving a substantial number of non-Africans in Africa.

Despite this ambiguity and subsequent confusion for the whole world, and Africans themselves, Africa has its fair share of non-Africans.

To compound the situation, there are more and more non-Africans coming to Africa providing mostly skilled labour for projects, NGO's and multi-nationals.

A good example of this complex situation is that of the recent Vice President and, after Sata's death, acting President of Zambia – Guy Scott. Scott was born in 1944 in Livingstone. It was then called Northern Rhodesia and is now Zambia. His father immigrated to Africa from Scotland in 1927 and his mother came from England in 1940. He is African.

To highlight the extent of non-Africans not being seen as African issue, here is an incident involving a super power. George W. Bush thought he was being pranked when Guy Scott was introduced as the Vice President of Zambia in a 2012 meeting. And this comes from a president who supports a number of charities in Zambia, so you'd think he'd know better.

Scott was acting President until replaced by the new President in April 2015.

About 5.5 million non-African people inhabit Africa. They are mostly Europeans of Dutch, French, German, British, Norwegian, Portuguese, Italian, Spanish, Greek and Irish descent. There are also Indian, Asian and Chinese populations throughout Africa. Although they only make up less than 1% of Africa's population they are significant in the skills they have brought and the contribution they make to Africa.

Travelling in Africa

Travel in Africa has been transformed over the last 20 years. The advent of the Internet changes the way that we find accommodation and allows potential travellers to search for this without the need for a travel agent. Bed and breakfasts, lodges, hotels and other providers now publish and advertise on the Internet for the new intrepid African explorers.

Dave Welmans

The major impact on travellers is the information available to explorers as well as their ability to still be connected almost wherever they go. This is a quantum leap away from travelling in Africa 20 years ago.

A traveller's best sources of additional information are guidebooks and local information from fellow travellers.

 Sites like AirBnb from San Francisco are also starting to change the way people come to Africa. It allows people to register as hosts to rent out lodging and the site allows users to leave reviews. This infiltration of technology is forever changing the Dark Continent from outside Africa.

But travelling in Africa can be a challenge. There is a lack of public transport, buses don't run on time and transport is almost always overcrowded. Coupled with immense heat, really bad roads and less than roadworthy vehicles, travelling can be a nightmare.

Africa is big! No make that HUGE. 3700km is the distance from San Francisco to New York. Travelling from the southern tip of Africa, you'd cover this distance 3 times before reaching Casablanca on the Atlantic.

7400km(4600mi) wide and 8000km (5000mi) long!

Open Africa promotes an eco-friendly authentic and local travel experience for travellers looking for a more immersive approach to travelling on the continent.

Travelling types in Africa

Africa has a number of classes of traveller:

At the top of the list is the luxury traveller with the 6-star hotels like the Serena Hotel in Nairobi. This will be the best hotel you'll ever stay in in the world, never mind Africa. At $2000 for a single room, it's not on everyone's budget, though.

A level down is the NGO and government officials' level, with expense accounts and business to do. $300-$500 is par for the course here.

The next level down is the average business traveller looking for opportunities and doing business on a budget in Africa. $200 is needed for a First World 3-star equivalent.

Further down is my favourite layer: the backpackers and idiosyncratic travellers layer. In sheer numbers these probably make up the bulk of Africa's travellers where $10-$50 will get you a bare but clean and functional room.

Dave Welmans

In all my travels in Africa, this is the most entertaining and enlightening group. Intrepid explorers from all over the world populate this layer in Africa. It is not uncommon for 10 different nationalities to be together in one place. Places like Cha-chas-chas in Lusaka, Steve's Place in Cape Maclear on Lake Malawi, Nungwe Village on Zanzibar Island, Njaya Lodge in Nkhata Bay (where I first got malaria) and the famous Doogles in Blantyre all cater for these travellers.

The next layer of travellers is the tight-budget traveller. Mostly relying on camping, these travellers are normally on extended trips – Cape to Cairo is popular. They normally do self-catering and keep the budget strings very tight.

The last level is the normal local traveller. This is the layer occupied mostly by the local inhabitants that rely on mass transportation systems like taxis and sometimes trucks, buses, pickups and tractors - the cheapest way of getting from A to B.

Once in Africa, most people will find themselves occupying a particular layer, but sometimes necessity will force you to upgrade or downgrade your layer.

I've been on the back of a pickup truck - that would normally carry 6 people in relative safety – with 26 other people holding on to each other to prevent a loss of a passenger. Another time, my travelling companion suffered sunstroke from the African sun.

If driving, you must be warned that traffic in Africa can be a nightmare. In Kampala, Lagos, Cairo or Nairobi it is normal for a trip of 10km to take an hour or more.

Border-crossing

The lack of regional integration in Africa is evident when crossing its borders. Travelling though Africa is probably the most daunting thing that foreigners will encounter and is compounded if they engage in cross-border trade.

Crossing a border in Africa is almost always a mission. Add to that a change in currency, a change in languages and even a change in the side of the road that you'll be driving on. It is these physical and political barriers that slow everything down in Africa.

"When we arrived at the border with Namibia, we weren't surprised to find out they wanted to fine us $150 dollars a day per person for every day we were over our limit. That meant that we were going to have to cough up $7500 as a group.
Finally, realising that we weren't going to be bullied by their threats, they did what they could to delay our progress leaving the country."
Brian Montalbo – BeyondAdventures

Customs duty is a large component of each country's income and the reliance on this income keeps these borders slow and arduous while providing petty bureaucrats with opportunities for graft. Added to this are the myriad of vaccinations, visas and permits needed for each African country. Each of these in term provide and opportunity for extortion and graft.

Commercial cross-border traffic is even worse with most border-crossings taking a number of days. Add to this, bad road infrastructure and lack of communication continues to hamper transport and logistics.

Dave Welmans

When transporting goods in Africa, technologies like satellites and Global Positioning Systems (GPS) can track the whereabouts of your car or cargo load. You may have difficulty getting there but at least you'll know where it is.

Shipping and containerisation
Containerisation is a system of freight transport using containers made of weathering steel. The containers have standardised dimensions. They can be loaded and unloaded, stacked, and transferred from one mode of transport to another - container ships, rail transport flatcars, and semi-trailer trucks - without being opened.

Containerisation has done away with the manual sorting of most shipments and the need for warehousing. Containerisation reduces congestion in ports, significantly shortening shipping time and reducing losses from damage and theft.

This containerisation has led to a 320% increase in bilateral trade in the world in its first 5 years of use and a further 320% over the last 20 years according to a report from Lunds University. This is more than the amount that they attribute to a bilateral free-trade agreement between countries. This means that containerisation contributes more to the global economy than all the trade agreements since 1945. Not bad for a simple box.

This containerisation allows goods to be moved easily via sea and then road with much less 'friction', which is a boon for all of Africa.

Uber

Once in a while a new way of doing business takes the world by storm. Such a storm is Uber.

The company uses a smartphone application to receive ride requests and then sends these trip requests to their drivers. Customers use the app to request rides and track their reserved vehicle's location. Despite not owning a vehicle or employing a driver, Uber is already valued at more than Avis and Budget car hire companies combined. Here is technology in the form of an app that is displacing a legacy transport system worldwide.

Currently, only 5 cities in Africa have the service, Cairo, Lagos and the 3 largest South African cities. This is a reflection of the relatively low number of smartphones in Africa today. But a statistic from Uber shows that more than 1m people used the service in South Africa in the first 6 months of 2015, reflecting the hugely disruptive nature of this business model.

This plays back into the better/cheaper driver of technology. A simple app puts the demand and supply side of metered taxi riding together.

Summary: Transport

The cosmopolitan nature of Africa is complex and confuses Africans and the rest of the world as to the use of the term 'African'.

The sheer size of Africa coupled with the 54 different countries with low levels of regional integration makes transport and logistics an opportunity for savvy minded business people. Anything that can help streamline this

Dave Welmans

industry will have a great impact in Africa. Despite this, there are hundreds of spectacular places to see and experience in Africa that will cause you to run this gauntlet.

Some places I'd put on your must see list:

Victoria Falls, Zambia and Zimbabwe
Kilimanjaro, Tanzania
Lakes - Lake Kariba, Malawi/Nyasa, Tanganyika, Victoria
Table Mountain, South Africa
The great migration, Tanzania
Mountain gorillas, Rwanda
Sahara dunes, Morocco
Pyramids of Giza, Egypt
Mount Mulanje, Malawi
Bazaruto Archipelago, Mozambique
Okavango Delta - Botswana
The Virunga Mountains - DRC/Rwanda/Uganda Borders
Ngorongoro Crater - Tanzania
Valley of the Kings, Egypt
Palais Namaskar, Marrakech, Morocco
Ifaty, Madagascar
Kruger National Park, South Africa
Lower Zambezi National Park, Zambia
Okavango Delta, Botswana
Stone Town, Tanzania
Lake Malawi National Park, Malawi

Dave Welmans

7. The Digital Revolution

Africa is late to the digital party. Technology is driven primarily by four factors and is adopted when it makes things:

- Quicker
- Cheaper
- Better

Markets are driven by a need to maximise production and minimise cost. They are all drivers of progress and this becomes the driver to adopt newer technologies. In some instances even though these three criteria aren't met, fashion or a strategic decision to use something may override the cost-production driver.

The Kalashnikov, or as it is more commonly known, the AK47, is the single most destructive piece of technology that has been introduced to Africa. Even today it is still the most commonly available weapon and is readily available

throughout Africa as the weapon of choice for insurgents, armies, rebels, criminals, law-enforcers and poachers. This Russian-designed weapon can be bought for as little as $10 in some countries.

The ubiquitous availability is somewhat a hangover from all the civil wars and independence movements from the late Sixties onwards. Soviet aligned countries shipped these cheap but deadly weapons in the millions to the armies involved in the struggles.

Not only were millions sent to Africa but also the nature of the weapon is so robust that even if it has been buried in mud for decades, once dug up is still functional. Africa has recycled these arms through generations and decades of changing political regimes.

The new AK47

The Nokia 1011 is the digital equivalent of the AK47 in the telecoms industry. It is ugly! It is heavy. But it worked and continues to work while changing Africa! Its numerous successors continue to change Africa too. I recently bought one of these bulletproof numbers for fun and the only thing that has changed in 20 years since they first became available is that under the battery it now says Microsoft Mobile! Ouch. A reminder that despite the initial success of Nokia, the advent of the smartphone in the form of the Android and Apple phones, disrupted this market enough to affect their profitability enough to allow Microsoft to gobble them up as part of *their* tech-strat approach to keeping a foothold in this space.

What being digital means

The digital revolution is going to have as big an impact in Africa as the AK47 but hopefully with more positive results.

The essence of being digital means that data or content is stored and transmitted in a digital or binary format, i.e. 0's

Dave Welmans

and 1's, while an analogue signal is the imprint of the raw vibration caused by the originating sound.

An excellent example is music. Originally music was recorded and reproduced by storing a waveform of the vibrations created by the music onto a storage medium that has evolved from wax to Bakelite to vinyl. Think of your normal vinyl record that has these vibrations stored and is reproduced by moving the needle across this imprint.

Once this waveform is converted to 0's and 1's, it can be stored more efficiently by using compression algorithms. The Compact Disc (CD) is an example of this digital storage. When music is stored in a digital format up to 150 songs can be stored on a single disc. This is about 10 times the amount available on a single analogue vinyl record. This is the benefit of going digital.

The next evolution of the CD is the Digital Versatile Disc (DVD) that can store up to 4 or 8 Gigabytes (GB) of data that replaced the CD and suddenly you could store a few thousand songs on a DVD. More than most people's total music collections.

DVDs ruled this space for a while as the price for the DVDs and the DVD reader/writers became cheaper until a newer technology in the form of the Universal Serial Bus (USB) or flash drive replaced the CD and DVD. This technology followed the same price reduction and capacity increase path as previous media options. Today software and large amounts of other data can be stored on these USB drives.

The largest commercial flash USB drive is a 1 Terabyte drive at around US $1100 in 2015. If you're reading this in a few years, these numbers will have already changed drastically.

What this means for Africa is that instead of shipping media, like songs and movies, on old-style storage systems like video cassette tapes and even newer DVDs, media can now be disseminated via a cheap USB flash drive. Add to this the ability to download or send the data across the Internet bypassing the need for the storage media entirely and we have a media revolution in the making.

The effect of technology in Africa, however, is not limited to computers and storage, but the transmission of information in telecoms has undergone the same revolution.

Between digital storage, digital processing and digital transmission life has been accelerating with all the added benefits of the effects of these devices following Moore's Law.

Moore's Law

Gordon E Moore was a co-founder of Intel, the semi-conductor giant, and his early observation (in 1965) that the rate at which technology in this field accelerates is known as Moore's Law.

"Moore's law" is the observation that, over the history of computing hardware, the number of transistors in a dense integrated circuit doubles approximately every two years.

Dave Welmans

Most digital and electronic devices reflect a strong correlation to Moore's Law: this affects the price and performance available to us in microprocessor prices, storage of data and RAM or memory capacity reflect this law.

We see this playing out in the dramatic improvement of the performance of electronics in every field. This law has described this accelerating improvement since first observed in 1965 and still holds true in 2015.

Intel executive David House refined Moore's Law finding that chip performance would double every 18 months.

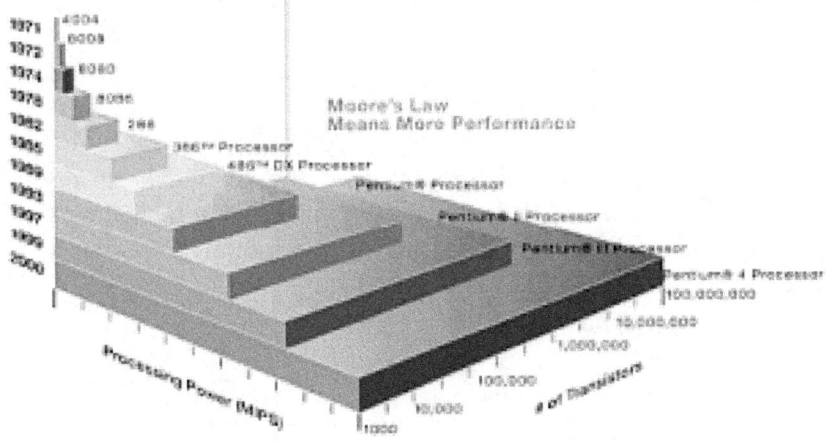

www.dailytech.com

Although seemingly only an interesting piece of information, this trend has had a radical effect that plays out in our everyday life.

Three important sectors driven by Moore's Law that have a large effect on our world are:

- Processor speed
- Storage
- Bandwidth

These three drivers continue to accelerate development in hardware and software and will continue to have an impact on the world and African lives.

This growth underpins the increase in processing power of applications available through the Internet. Companies like Google make extensive use of these accelerating drivers to bring new and better applications to the world. Google Earth is an interesting example. The application uses an Internet connection and provides satellite imagery covering the whole world. A user does not need to resort to buying specialised and expensive maps of their region but can capitalise on the 'free' digital world of Google Earth and Google Maps.

The extra bonus to this application is the ground breaking Google Street View. Unfortunately, it has a limited coverage in African cities. The following African countries have a number of cities on Google Street View:

- Botswana
- Egypt
- Lesotho
- South Africa
- Swaziland
- Tanzania
- Madeira and The Azores
- The Canary Islands

That's only 8 countries out of 54. Now if Google Street View hasn't got there yet, it remains Darkest Africa.

Dave Welmans

Death of the printed word

An example of the devastating impact of digitisation is in the field of a digital storage of information. The written and then the printed word are hailed as one of mankind's greatest achievements - until the Internet. The Internet first started encroaching on this space soon to be followed by the ability to find it, perfected pretty much by the Google search engine. The search giant first started battering the physical storage of information with their search engine that made its easy and relevant answers a strong contender to knock out the encyclopaedia.

The final blow to the printed encyclopaedia came from Wikipedia, an open-source consumer-written encyclopaedia of knowledge that is free and easy to access through any Internet connection. It is more up to date and holds more current and relevant information than almost any other store of knowledge. School kids now use Wikipedia as their source of information and not the *Encyclopaedia Britannica* in libraries as was the case in the past. William Kamkwamba would have a field day.

Reducing friction

In his 1996 book, *The Road Ahead*, Bill Gates writes of "friction-free capitalism," a type of marketplace that he argues will be ushered in by the spread of Internet-style electronics.

One of the differentiating factors between the First and Third Worlds is the amount of economic friction that exists in the economy. First World countries already inhabit what has become a remarkably low-friction economy while Africa is still slowed down by this economic friction.

Economic friction is everything that keeps markets from working according to the textbook model of perfect competition: Distance. Cost. Restrictive regulations. Imperfect information.

In African high-friction markets, customers don't have options to choose between many suppliers. The location of a store is a great part of its success. You literally own the space and it becomes harder for new competitors to steal market share, unless they take the trouble to move into the same location. This traditional way of business makes the markets move slowly and predictably. High-tech digital and hence, low-friction markets, are just the opposite. A new competitor can spring up literally anywhere in the world and compete with local suppliers. It is also much easier for customers to swap their suppliers. This makes high-tech digital businesses anything but predictable.

As Gates noted in 1995, this reduction in the economics of business over the past 20 years has been the enormous reduction in friction that has affected all industries. This is also the underlying driver of globalisation that allow companies to reduce friction and create industries with less or low friction.

This creeping globalisation has opportunities for Africans, giving them access to information and, having developed products, access to markets for these products.

Linus shows the way
The open-source movement has made a large contribution to the reduction of economic friction and the advancement of

technology throughout the world through a culture of sharing and collaborative development.

This has a particularly large impact on Africa where access to information has always been limited or came at an exorbitant cost. How does a person living below the breadline afford to buy Microsoft Office to type up her proposal or CV? The open-source movement with Libre Office and Open Office are the answers to this problem.

The open-source movement has a lot to thank in Linus Torvalds, who produced the original PC-based version of Linux.

Although the open-source approach was nothing new in 1994, as companies like Ford and IBM had all had some success with this approach in the past, it was Linus Torvalds' release of a brilliant operating system to run on PCs that helped catapult open-source into a serious game-changing technology.

On 14 March 1994, the first public version of Linux was released. This was a Unix-type operating system that was now available on the PC platform. It was a migration from the corporate mainframe environment into the consumer-accessible PC world.

The importance of this release is both the brilliance of the operating system code and the 'free' use of the operating system that allows anybody to make use of and contribute to its development and improvement. Linus chose the open-source route as his tech-strat approach: an approach that pays huge dividends.

Linux was originally developed as an operating system for Intel x86–based personal computers, but due to its performance and availability has been used to drive almost every device that exists today. It is now the most widely used operating system in the world.

It is now the leading operating system on PC's, servers and mainframe computers. It is also the operating system of choice for supercomputers. 99% of Internet-connected routers and servers run Linux.

The combination of the availability of the cheaper PC and a freely available, constantly improving, operating system and ecosystem of applications makes this world of technology a fast changing place. The beauty is that Linux is the same in Helsinki or New York or Bujumbura.

Previously only the domain of geeks who knew how to code and who sat in dark basements around the world, the newer versions of Linux have user-friendly Graphical User Interfaces (GUI's).

We all have a bit of Linux in our lives! Linux is pervasive even if you've never seen or heard of it. It runs on embedded systems, which are purpose-specific devices: mobile phones or tablets run Linux, normally the Google specific version called Android. Android, which is now the most widely used operating system for tablets and smartphones is built on top of the Linux kernel.

This open-source development of Linux is the most successful example of free and open-source software collaboration. It is called open-source because the original source code is usually available for other developers to further develop modifications of that software as long as they then release these improvements back into the open-source community. The underlying source code may be used, modified, and

Dave Welmans

distributed - commercially or non-commercially - by anyone under license of the GNU (General Public License).

The biggest problem is that this feedback and further development or modifications leads to something called forking does lead to a dizzying amount of versions for people to choose from. Popular Linux distributions include Debian, Ubuntu, Linux Mint, Fedora, openSUSE, Arch Linux, and the commercial Red Hat Enterprise Linux and SUSE Linux Enterprise Server. For all the Apple Macintosh fans out there, the Mac OS is built on top of BSD – a version of Linux.

Open-source computers
The open-source movement is now infiltrating the hardware world. The impact and future of this way of sharing knowledge is a major driver for advancing collective knowledge and a quicker development cycle throughout the world but has particular benefit for Africa that has long suffered from being excluded from access to knowledge and expertise.

A good example of this open-source movement working together is, for example, the Raspberry Pi computer and the Arduino controller board. The Raspberry Pi provides the computing power for the application and the Arduino controller deals with the interface to the physical world with digital and analogue inputs and outputs. This provides a great development platform and removes the need to develop the hardware as well as the software for an application.

The open-source fraternity actively encourages users to re-contribute their own development to the community and this secondary benefit becomes an online mentoring and development environment that sounds perfect for Africa.

Open-source has helped the lower cost of production for Raspberry Pi's that are sold for $35 and the Arduino controller boards for $20.

The Raspberry Pi is a powerful credit-card sized computer that runs, of course, open-source versions of Linux. It can be powered by a USB power source. Some versions come with the open-source Libre Office (or it can be downloaded free) and this added functionality makes this a pretty good and functional PC.

A low-cost open-source computer is a boon to the lagging African developer. If you need more computing power – just slap a number of these babies into a Linux-cluster and you're approaching the power of a supercomputer at the cost of a standard Dell laptop.

This low-cost power-packed 'PC' has sold over 4.5m devices since 2012 and over a million of the latest incarnation in just 2 months.

Dave Welmans

The Raspberry Pi is a brilliant example of how the open-source community can out-develop the commercial world and deliver a PC on a stick-sized computer at a phenomenal price.

For the interface between the digital world and the physical world, the Arduino controller board has arrived. It is produced by Arduino, an open-source computer hardware and software company including project and user communities. They design kits for building these smart devices by being interactive and can sense and interact with the physical world.

The Arduino boards basically provide a set of digital and analogue input/output pins that can be controlled to manage various processes and environments.

For developers, there is a serial interface for loading programs developed on possibly the Raspberry Pi. The first

Arduino was introduced in 2005. Over 1 million of these boards have been sold to date.

These boards are used for developing untold new applications from smart home systems to drones to 3-D printers. Many of them run on this board.

This is an example of open-source development and what it could mean to Africa. You can hook up a knitting machine to a computer and download styles and knit them. Seriously!

Easy as that. Build a drone. Build a 3-D printer. With access to the designs and access to a PC-controlled machine, almost anything can be produced. Imagine the latest Daniel Hechter design being reproduced in Mogadishu!

The obvious and profound effects of these open-source projects, both hardware and software, allow Africans to catch up to - if not leapfrog - their counterparts around the world.

First, the growing access to the Internet means that people can find things like this. Second, once found they now don't have to pay for the use of these designs. The barrier to entry is all but removed. This short-circuits so many problems that slow down development in Africa.

If you want to build a device that tracks the direction of the sun to optimise solar photovoltaic (PV) use, you don't have to first become proficient in building controller boards but can leverage off both the above-mentioned open-source hardware platforms. Even better yet, someone probably has done a similar project and shared it on an open-source platform.

Dave Welmans

Now a kid in Ghana and a student in Kenya can both build businesses around the production and implementation of these systems for the betterment of their communities.

The digital divide

The digital divide is a term coined to describe the economic and social chasm that exists between different populations. This description includes the access to information and knowledge of information and communication technologies (ICT).

The difference between countries on the positive side of this technology chasm and those on the downside is called the Digital Divide.

From the outset, Africa has been on the wrong side of this chasm. It has been the subject of much research as to how to lessen this impact or bridge the digital divide.

The combination of open-source hardware and software communities is the light at the end of the tunnel for Africa. The open-source movement has moved away from proprietary royalties and allows everybody basically free access to both the use and further development of these items.

Think of this: It costs around $300 for a copy of Microsoft Office, and every upgrade attracts more licensing fees. For Africans, a bootleg copy is often the only option. Today, royalty-free versions of open-source productivity tools like Libre Office deliver very similar functionality at a zero licensing cost.

Fledgling companies in the late 1990s such as Red Hat, Suse, and Google, and those that have arrived since, such as

Canonical and many others, have become enormous open-source success stories. Industry titans such as IBM and Sun have also embraced the open-source approach. Once viewed with suspicion, this open-source development has been widely adopted across industries. Companies are moving at varying rates away from trying to develop their own eco-systems and now rely on open-source software to accelerate their own development cycles.

Clouds on the horizon

What do you do if you need to develop an application that needs high-end computing but don't have the capital or access to these devices? You look to the clouds.

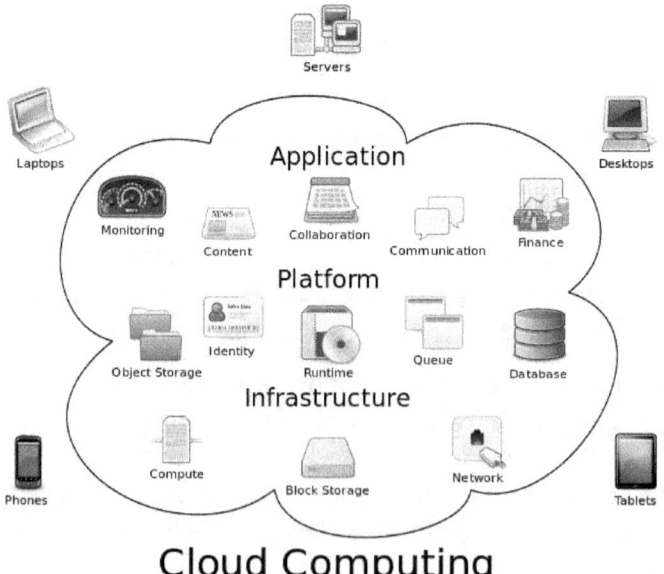

Cloud Computing

Wikipedia

Dave Welmans

The ability to use computing power stored somewhere on the Internet is called cloud computing. Since the dawn of the Internet, a limited form of this has existed but its use has now reached critical mass. Previously, applications like Gmail and Facebook were examples of cloud applications. Today, almost anything can be moved to the cloud. The first requirement is obviously a connection from the user to the cloud-based service or application. Business applications can be better run and managed once they exist in the cloud. Centralised data centres allow for a single point of management while the software allows for redundancy and scalability on demand.

As a company, it makes more sense to focus on your core competencies and not to have to worry about how your bits and bytes are being harnessed, protected and backed-up.

It also allows a low-cost start-up to utilise shared resources rather than the need to invest in the capital required for computing equipment needed by most companies. The advent of the cloud allows a quick, easy and relatively cheap start-up of applications and services – a recipe for Africa.

Virtualisation
An advance that dovetails into this cloud technology is the advancement in Virtualisation Technology. This virtualised machine (VM) provides an ability to run a virtual server/application on top of another virtual operating system that is dynamically scaled and managed by this virtualisation platform. This may sound slightly redundant but the size and computing power allocated to these virtual machines can be scaled almost immediately and dynamically. It also allows for an aggregated use of the technology instead of multiple

physical servers taking up lots of power and space standing idle for most of the time.

This aggregation of computing power lends itself very well to cloud computing. A tablet/phone is a good example of using cloud technology for applications and allowing the heavy lifting to be done in the cloud while the device is used for input and display. This combination of cloud and virtualised technology provides the perfect environment for companies to quickly roll out and scale applications.

Now people can run business applications for a fraction of the previously capital-intensive cost. This lowers the barrier to entry and sets up opportunities for more people to get their start-ups off the ground.

Internet of Things and big data

The proliferation of Internet-connected devices (think fridges, cars, phones) and the information that they collectively produce is known as the Internet of Things (IoT). The information being generated on the Internet is following an exponential growth and will grow 500% in the next 5 years.

Consider that the world creates as much data in 2 days as was created from the dawn of mankind until 2003. The ability to extract meaningful data from these very large data sets is what Big Data is all about.

"Every two days now we create as much information as we did from the dawn of civilization up until 2003. That's something like five Exabytes of data."

Eric Schmidt, Google.

Dave Welmans

The storage of all this collective data (think Facebook) allows this data to be 'mined' for information. The advent of the explosion of information that will be generated by the IoT will also add to the value of this data.

Africa is being left behind in this field and will only join the Big Data revolution once it is meaningfully connected.

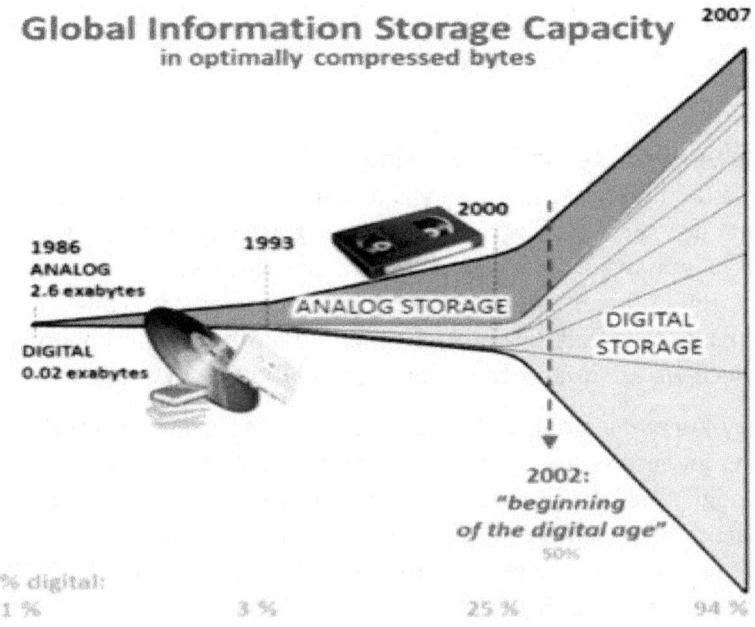

Hilbert, M., & López, P. (2011). The World's Technological Capacity to Store, Communicate, and Compute Information.

Digital vs Analogue: % of total 2007;

19 Exabytes = 6% Analogue

- Paper, film, audiotapes, vinyl, old VHS tapes

280 Exabytes = 94% Digital

- 11.2% - flashdrives, CD's
- 8.9% - computer server/mainframes
- 22% - DVD/Blu-Ray
- 44.5% - PC Hard drives

Beware the technological singularity

The technological singularity is a name given to a hypothesis that accelerating progress in technologies will eventually lead to a runaway effect where artificial intelligence (AI) will exceed human intelligence. The reason it is called a singularity is that, like a black hole, it denotes a point beyond which we are unable to see or predict what might happen.

Ray Kurzweil is one of the fathers of AI and is also a futurist and inventor while his day job is as director of engineering at Google. He writes extensively on the future of technology, particularly robotics and AI. From his well-informed viewpoint, he predicts that the Technological Singularity will take place by 2045.

The world takes notice of what Kurzweil says if only for the fact that he accurately predicted at what stage computers would be able to beat the best chess player in the world. It happened in 1997 when IBM's Big Blue beat Gary Kasparov, 3 years before the turn of the century.

The next big hurdle to catch the human imagination was having a computer win on a game show. In 2011, Watson –

Dave Welmans

the name given to the IBM supercomputer – beat other previous winners to win the $1m prize.

How this is going to impact on Africa remains to be seen but it is conceivable that telecoms, supercomputers and the Internet may, for example, supplement Médecins Sans Frontières (MSF) and bring much-needed expertise via the Internet to parts of Africa that have very little medical capability.

At some point, these autonomous machines will quickly pass our limited intelligence and we will find ourselves in a situation where we are no longer the brightest beings on the planet.

If managed correctly, this super intelligence will be the biggest technological impact that mankind will ever see, even if it may be the last. The preferred scenario is that this/these super intelligent 'beings' will help us plan and implement all the steps necessary for mankind's progress. They could help plan how to manage and adapt our rapacious use of fossil fuels and water.

Leaving behind our new super-intelligent overlords, the next chapter focuses on digital media and its impending impact on Africa.

Summary: The Digital Revolution
- The world is becoming a digital world.
- Moore's Law shows the exponential growth of the performance of the digital-based technology.
- The need to be quicker, cheaper and better drives the adoption of technology.
- Technology helps reduce economic friction.

- Open-source development of hardware and software is a sound business strategy.
- Africans can collaborate with information and technology through this ecosystem.
- Cloud computing and virtualisation are a means for Africa to neutralise their computer disadvantage.
- Data creation is exploding with more data being created every 2 days than was created in mankind's entire history up to 2003.
- The Technological Singularity is where computers will be smarter that mankind.

8. Media

Do you remember the Betamax video player? The tape deck or Sony Walkman? Then you're old enough to understand that since the 1970s and the advent of television broadcasting in Africa, things have changed. This change is global and driven by many factors, but the effect and impact of this change in technology has an impact on people and the way that they consume media content today.

The development of storage and playback devices and technology has changed dramatically over the years. From Betamax to MP4 format on a USB flash disk. We've gone from VHS videocassettes to Personal Video Recorders (PVRs) and streaming IP Television.

"Digitisation is fundamentally reshaping business models. It is lowering barriers to entry and expanding market reach for enterprises."

Joseph Tegbe
Management Consulting Advisory

The move to digital storage and transmission of content from documents, music and video allows for non-specific devices to play all these different content types. No longer are people stuck with a large immovable television that could barely pick up the analogue transmission of the country's local broadcast. This 'dumb' device could only do that.

Today, a smart TV is Internet-connected and has the ability to store and play almost any content. It will also play a movie stuck onto a USB flash drive. The 'bad' old days required an analogue version of dubious quality and origin on a video tape as well as another 'dumb' device, the video player, to be able to enjoy the content.

Today in Africa, content may well be available through a satellite broadcast provider and, to make things more convenient, consumers can decide to record or store the content to be enjoyed when they choose.

Broadcasters and telecoms service providers are seeing a huge upswing in data usage because of this digital migration.

Steve Jobs and iTunes

One of Steve Jobs' greatest contributions to technology and the world was the creation of the iPod. People remember Jobs for his later developments, but it really started with the iPod. This was revolutionary on a number of fronts.

The first impact of the iPod is that Jobs helped move the world from analogue-stored audio like the vinyl record to a digital and portable storage medium. This digital storage and music player put paid to the likes of the Sony Walkman and Discman.

The second achievement was the storage format in the form of the Apple Audio Codec (AAC). This wasn't the first digital music player, but it was the one that gained enough critical mass to attract the mainstream and not just the fringe of geeks, nerds and technophiles.

The third impact and possibly a more revolutionary achievement was Jobs' ability to persuade the major content providers like Sony to allow their content to be available in a digital format.

This was particularly impressive since it came at a time the Napster was at its peak. Napster was a controversial music-sharing company that was eventually closed down due to copyright infringement.

This achievement enabled the creation and spread of iTunes as a precursor for the Apple App store. This hurdle must not be underestimated. The ability to persuade the paranoid Burbank copyright lawyers to let some of this content out of their control was unprecedented.

Jobs managed to do this by building a version of Digital Rights Management (DRM) that he used as a means to ensure the prevention of digital duplication of the music. It was an essential step needed to persuade the lawyers to embrace the new ecosystem.

Jobs later removed this DRM as it transpired that people pirate music more out of a desire to have the music in bit/byte size pieces and at a cheap rate (a single song typically went for US9c and a whole album for US$1) than wanting the music for free. The success of the iTunes store is legendary and has helped shaped the explosive digital distribution of content.

Finally, the digitisation of this content paved the way for other content, e.g. movies and television, to be similarly distributed.

The next globe-shaking development from Apple came in the form of the iPhone. Again, not the original smartphone, but transformative enough to help accelerate and define the standard for smartphones and destroy the 'dumb' and feature phone as well as the world's largest smartphone maker, Blackberry, at the time.

I mention Blackberry, as it was the first smartphone to gain substantial market share in Africa and still today, in 2015, retains a substantial market share of the smartphone market in Africa, even though Blackberry seems to have a limited lifespan at the moment.

The development of the iPhone opened and helped create the ecosystem for smartphones over feature phones and unlock the enormous potential that smartphones can bring to Africa.

The wind-up radio

Arthur Goldstuck reports in an article on Gadget.co.za:

"Back in 1993, inventor Trevor Baylis was watching a TV show about the spread of AIDS in Africa, and learned that in many parts of the continent radio was the only means of communication. But even a basic radio represented a major obstacle: the cost of batteries."

The cost of batteries was the first hurdle while the ability to re-charge the batteries or have access to electricity was another. In an effort to solve this particular Third World problem, Baylis created a clockwork mechanism to overcome these hurdles. He created a radio that would provide cheap power, but, unfortunately the device itself was hardly cheap. It would cost around $40 for the cheapest model in South Africa, and up to $75 elsewhere in Africa, which is out of the reach of most of Africa's poor.

Despite this mismatch of product with a market, Baylis' radio still became iconic with over 3m devices in circulation. Even

Dave Welmans

though his tech-strat approach was flawed, he was lucky enough to still reach a big enough market.

Transforming home lighting in Africa is possible with the same simple clockwork design combined with low energy LED lights. A further enhancement would be to couple a photovoltaic (PV) panel onto the device. See below in the chapter on energy.

Nollywood

The cinema of Nigeria, often referred to as Nollywood was established in the just before the turn of the century and grew to become the second largest film industry in the world in number of annual film productions, placing it ahead of the US and behind only India.

In 2013, it was rated as the third most valuable film industry in the world after generating a revenue of US$10bn in 2013 alone, placing it behind India and the USA.

These movies don't go to theatres but mostly get released directly to video. This is content made by Africans for Africans. Nollywood generates more movies than Hollywood.

The business model dictates that production costs must be low and sales volumes must be high for this model to be sustainable. This seems to be working well for Nollywood. Nigerian films outsell Hollywood films in Nigeria and many other African countries. Africa seems to be taking a very different approach to that of Hollywood or even Bollywood, one with its high budget driven productions and the other with specific Indian cultural content. These Nollywood producers turn out movies at an astonishing rate with some producing a new movie every week. The distribution model is through Nigerian shops and market stalls where a reasonable title will sell up to 50 000 copies. The better performing titles can reach sales of a few hundred thousand. Due to the low cost of production, the videos are sold for $1 to $2 each, allowing most Nigerians to purchase them. The speed of the industry also prevents pirating having a considerable effect on their profitability. In all, more than 1200 films a year are produced in Nigeria.

The Nigerian films are better received by the market in Africa when compared to foreign films probably due to cost and availability as well as the cultural bias that reflects African society. People seem to prefer to watch shows representative of their own cultures.

Digital TV (DTTV)

You have to love techies for their acronyms! DTTV stands for Digital Terrestrial Television and it has made a lot of noise lately and possibly rightfully so. The way DTTV works as compared to normal analogue TV broadcast is that the signal has been converted to a digital format, which is one aspect that allows further advancement in the way of compression and storage. The second and more important factor is that it converts a relatively inefficient signal broadcast to one with a much smaller spectral footprint.

In 2006, the International Telecommunications Union decided that all countries in Europe, Africa, Middle East and Iran should migrate from analogue to digital broadcasting to free up bandwidth. The deadline set was 2015 and only two countries in Africa met this deadline, but most other countries are in process to this migration.

Dave Welmans

Once a country rolls out DTTV it can reclaim and recycle the spectrum that was being used by the original broadcast for other uses – think broadband and cellular technology.

DTT is a terrestrial based distribution model differing from the satellite broadcast model. The TV signal is broadcast from a number of towers that can also allow two-way communication.

This system requires a set top box (STB) to decode the signal, similarly to a satellite broadcast. Through this broadcast connection, the modem or router can also provide two-way communication on the same frequency being used by the TV broadcast.

The use of the set top box also allows a connection back to the Internet for users. This link is going to be slow, but at least it is more than the most people have already.

Further to this improvement is the advent of a technology called TV White Space (TVWS). The aim of this technology is to allow the use this broadcast spectrum to be shared with a communication access network.

The basis for this technology is that the analogue signals need to have more space between channels to avoid interference and work effectively, while a digital signal can be confined to a very specific range without bleed into neighbouring channels. The equipment will dynamically channel hop to avoid interference if any TV signal is detected in the area. This means that an Internet connection co-exists with the same spectrum being used for TV broadcasts.

Both Microsoft and Google have pilot projects running in Kenya and South Africa testing this technology. In the real world, this translates to a wireless signal that can travel much further than normal wireless but has limited throughput potential. These characteristics make it ideal for rural deployment of low bandwidth intensive application or access.

iRokoTV

The ongoing digitisation of the storage and delivery of media provides new business opportunities. iRokoTV is a new company that has created a platform to provide pay per view Nigerian films on demand. It is one of Africa's first online movie-streaming websites. They have a catalogue of over 5000 Nollywood film titles. This young company has shown that IPTV already has a place in Africa.

iRokoTV was started in 2011 by Jason Njoku's, iRoko Partners and has become one of the fastest growing Internet companies in Nigeria.

Within 6 months of launch, iRokoTV had generated 3m visits from visitors based in 178 countries. One of the major keys to this success has been the increase in Internet speeds on the continent. This increase was greater than a factor of 100 between 2008 and the launch of the service. Added to this is the drop in the cost of connectivity in Nigeria that has fallen by a factor of 40. Together they provide the business case environment for the ongoing growth of the service.

Having moved to a digital platform distributed across the Internet means that the service is not constrained to Nigeria but is accessible anywhere else in the world. There are more people that use the service in London than they do in the whole of Nigeria.

Dave Welmans

This is a great case for an African digital export that has adopted a technologically advanced strategy that is paying off.

Amazon
Amazon.com started as an online bookstore started in 1994 by Jeff Bezos. It soon started selling electronics, clothing, toys and jewellery amongst others. They are also a manufacturer of electronic goods, one of which is the Kindle, an e-book reader. The Kindle is rightfully seen as the iPhone of e-book readers as it was the device that brought this way of reading into the mainstream.

Not so well known outside the states is that Amazon was also one of the first companies to deliver consumer accessible cloud computing on a Web Service and Cloud Computing platform.

In the book realm, Amazon sold to all 50 states in America and shipped to another 45 countries. His choice of strategy was going to pay off big time. Even though they were the biggest online bookstore almost overnight, they had the advantage of not even having to hold a single book in stock. Where bookstores would have to order and hold stock, Amazon could hold a virtual stock of unlimited quantities. They paid their rent for their digital presence and soon outperformed the brick and mortar bookstores.

The resilience of their strategy became apparent when Amazon thrived while many digital companies failed to survive the dotcom bubble burst. Jeff Bezos was named Time magazine's man of the year in 1999.

Jeff Bezos had set up a brilliant tech-strat approach to his business. Amazon was an Internet-focussed technology company that soon focussed on all aspects of providing access to goods and services through his company.

Further to the retailing, they pick markets that typically are less efficient and can be replaced by a more efficient digital version of that business and develop these solutions and products.

The core technology that keeps Amazon running is Linux-based. As of 2005, Amazon had the world's three largest Linux databases.

The direct benefit of Amazon to Africans is that almost any book can be sourced and delivered over the Internet. Africans are being released from location-based libraries and are now able to access the whole world of printed media.

A further, and possibly more important, reason to feature Amazon here is that they are also the world's largest cloud computing platform, which will become increasingly important to Africa Start-ups.

Although this is an American company that has embraced technology and continues to disrupt traditional business models, they remain a perfect case study for Africans.

Dave Welmans

CreateSpace

Amazon continues to use the new digital world to displace the old analogue one. This book was written and initially published through an Amazon subsidiary called CreateSpace.

CreateSpace is a print-on-demand publishing service that enables small fry (like me) to write and publish a book without the need for a physical publisher. This reduces the need for aspiring African writers to first secure the backing of a publisher before releasing a book on the world. The next great African Steinbeck novel may well come out of a corner of Africa.

eBooks

There are platforms like Kindle, Barnes & Noble, Apple and a few other digital eBook publishers. Now libraries and bookshops exist more online than in the physical world.

For Africa, the smartphones and tablets will be the new e-readers for these books. The proportion of all books sold in the U.S. that are Kindle titles amounts to 19.5%. E-books now make up around 30% of all book sales, and Amazon has a 65% share within that category,

Torrents

The new digital world encourages new and clever ways of transmitting digital media and underpins the growth in the digital revolution. One of the protocols that have been developed is the BitTorrent file sharing protocol.

Programmer Bram Cohen designed the protocol in April 2001 and released the first version on 2 July 2001. It is currently estimated that up to 70% of all traffic on the Internet makes use of this peer-to-peer file sharing protocol.

Here's how it works. A file is created, the descriptor or index file, and is uploaded to a torrent site. This descriptor file is a dynamic file that is constantly updated by all the users accessing the file. The initial file distributor is known as the seeder.

People wanting to download the file first download the descriptor that keeps an index of all copies of the file available at that point in time and allows users, known as peers or leechers, to download portions of this file from other users downloading the same file.

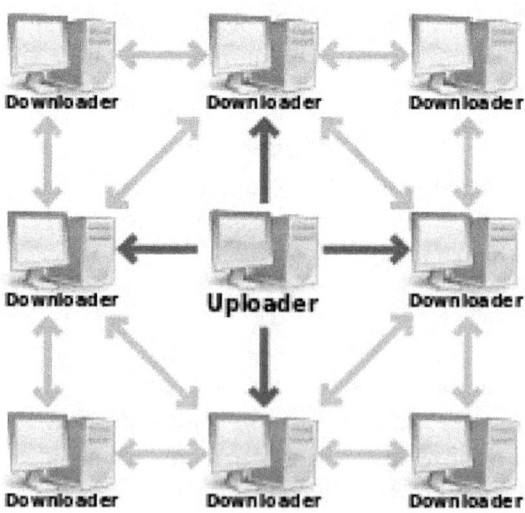

Dave Welmans

An example of how popular this way of distributing content is the latest *Game of Thrones* season that had up to 193 000 people sharing the second episode and 2m people downloaded this episode within 24 hours of its airing.

With this technology, it is as likely that *Game of Thrones* has a great African audience even if it isn't being broadcast in Africa.

Television as birth control

In the chapter on economics and finance, we touched on food insecurity and explosive population growth in Africa. Despite the view that Africa can possibly increase food production by 5 times over the medium-term future, there is still a large risk of continued food shortages. Food security and population growth are on a collision course over the next few decades but technology in the form of television brings with it some positivity.

NUMBER OF CHILDREN UNDER 18 BY UNICEF REGION

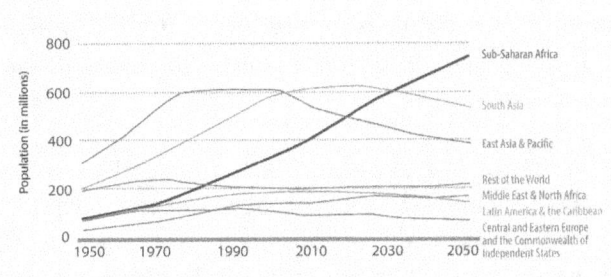

Source:UNICEF (2012), Generation 2025 and Beyond.

Studies show that the availability of television curbs population growth – well documented in Mexico and India. Whatever the reasons for this – and the studies are complex - it is important to note that the availability of basic television will start to slow population growth in Africa.

Television's spread throughout the world is pervasive. In Asia and Latin America, even the poorest are glued to the box. In Africa, however, the spread has been slower. Given a population exceeding a billion, there are only around 50m TV sets – a penetration of less than 0.5%. Mostly government sponsored, television broadcasting in Africa is mostly amateurish and unattractive and satellite dishes to access other satellite broadcaster remain rare outside southern Africa. The radio is still the primary entertainment and news device.

This technology could be a catalyst for change. In Kenya, there is a TV soap called *Makutano Junction*, funded by a foreign NGO. It works in conjunction with a family planning clinic and is now in its successful 12th series. The viewership for this soapie is impressive with 7m viewers tuning in from Kenya and many more in Tanzania and Uganda.

Since the launch of the show in 2001, the fertility rate in Kenya has fallen by almost 40%. This does not mean that it is this show that has the responsibility of reducing the population growth, but it is apparent that the soapie does help educate and inform the population of choices and services available that in turn have led to this decline.

Dave Welmans

The impact of television on population growth is complex with reasons ranging from education concerning health and fertility to changing cultural attitudes and can also just be the reduction in time spent in bed that contributes to this decline.

The two-way digital street
The digital platform that now exists worldwide allows both the access to information and entertainment but, almost more importantly for Africans, also allows a platform to begin contributing to the digital stores of information in YouTube, iTunes and the like.

A smartphone-captured video of a Ghanaian singer might be the next Justin Bieber of the Internet. At the same time, it affords a forum for public expression, which is often needed in Africa.

Nollywood may just learn a trick and start using this digital video platform to start delivering content similar to iRokoTV thereby expanding its market to a worldwide one immediately. The business model just has to change to become sustainable on the revenue generated from this advertising driven platform.

Movies and books about Africa
Below are some of my favourite movies and books about Africa. Reading these books and watching these movies will paint a background picture of Africa that is mostly accurate and informative. They cover a wide range of subjects – some closer to reality than others - and span many different decades in Africa. Some are historical and others are

fictional, but all have a good view of their part of the African Elephant.

Movies	Books
Blood Diamond	*Things Fall Apart* - Chinua Achebe
The Constant Gardener	*The Poisonwood Bible* - Barbara Kingsolver
Hotel Rwanda	*Uhuru* – Leon Uris
Cry the Beloved Country	*The No1 Ladies' Detective Agency* - Alexander McCall Smith
Mandela: Long Walk to Freedom	*Disgrace* - J M Coetzee
Out of Africa	*Cry, the Beloved Country* - Alan Paton
Tears of the Sun	*A Dry White Season* - André P Brink
Tsotsi	*Long Walk to Freedom: The Autobiography* - Nelson Mandela
The Last King of Scotland	*A Far Off Place* – Laurens Van Der Post
The First Grader	*Jock of the Bushveld* – Percy Fitzpatrick
Gorillas in the Mist	*Gorillas in the Mist* – Dian Fossey
Shaka Zulu	*Born Free* – Joy Adamson
Invictus	*Power of One* – Bryce Courtenay
Searching for Sugarman	*Heart of Darkness* – Joseph Conrad
The English Patient	*Around Africa on my Bike* & *Around Madagascar on My Kayak* - Riaan Manser
Lord of War	*Spud* – John Van De Ruit
Sarafina	
	The Story of an African Farm – Olive Schreiner

Dave Welmans

The Gods must be Crazy	*King Solomon's Mines* – Sir H. Rider Haggard
Zulu Dawn	*Mafeking Road* & *Stone Cold Jug* – Herman Charles Bosman
Spud	*Dark Continent, My Black Arse* – Sihle Khumalo
Mountains of the Moon	*King Leopold's Ghost* – Adam Hochschild
I am Slave	*Africa – in the footsteps of the Great Explorers* - Kinglsey Holgate
Black Hawk Down	*Lonely Planet* – Lonely Planet Guides
Captain Phillips	*China Safari* - Sege Michel Michel Beuret
Amistad	*Riotous Assembly* – Tom Sharpe
The Ghost and the Darkness	*River God* – Wilbur Smith
Ghandi	*White Mischief* – James Fox

Summary: Media

The status of media has evolved radically over the last few decades. Between new ways of delivering content and new devices that combine different forms of media the face of media is almost unrecognisable.

Connectivity coupled with smart devices allows over the top (OTT) services like IP streaming to change the way that we consume our media. Gone are the days where you'd rush home to catch the 8pm news bulletin from your one-channel analogue TV broadcast.

Today, people decide what they want to watch and when they want to watch it. And the best thing is that all this technology allows us to skip those pesky adverts.

In conclusion to this chapter:

- The world and Africa is becoming digital.
- Steve Jobs helped launch digital storage of media.
- Nollywood is Africa's Hollywood.
- Amazon and CreateSpace are examples of digital media companies.
- EBooks are still gaining traction.
- Torrents are the most popular method for distributing large media files, particularly movies and music.
- TV reduces population growth.
- New digital platforms afford Africans a chance to be exposed to the rest of the world.

The previous chapters on the effect of accelerating technology development together with the digitisation of the world, especially media, lay the foundation for the real technological revolution that is taking place in Africa.

I will explain the initial wave of the communications revolution and how access to the Internet in the form of broadband is about to engulf and change Africa.

The next chapter examines how telecoms is having an effect in Africa.

Dave Welmans

9. Telecoms

Telecoms can be divided into two major sectors: voice connectivity and data or broadband connectivity. The need for voice communications has driven cellphone adoption in Africa to date, but it is the coming broadband revolution on the back of these cellular networks that will drive the next technological revolution in Africa.

Several studies have demonstrated that broadband penetration is an important factor for economic growth and nowhere more so than in developing countries, particularly Africa.

The World Bank reports that a 10% increase in broadband correlates to a 1.38% increase in GDP growth.

Extending reach and increasing impact, 2009

The broadband penetration sweeping Africa will translate into substantial growth. The title of this book was influenced by the technological change sweeping through Africa bringing connectivity to the last billion people on the planet.

The definition of Broadband by the Federal Communications Commission (FCC) in 2010 was a minimum speed of 4 Mbps download and 1 Mbps upload. This has recently been updated to 25 Mbps download and 4 Mbps upload in February 2015.

Even if Africa's broadband connectivity fails First World definitions, it is still simply the availability of a connection to the Internet that is at the heart of the new African digital revolution. Africa's broadband revolution is coming, even if slower than the rest of the world. Similarly to the way cellphones filled a need, access to the Internet fills a similar vacuum in Africa.

It is the growth in this technology that is at the heart of the technological wave that is connecting the Last Billion.

Africa differs from the First World when it comes to their telecoms roadmap and is following a slightly different path in its evolution to maturity.

Undersea cables

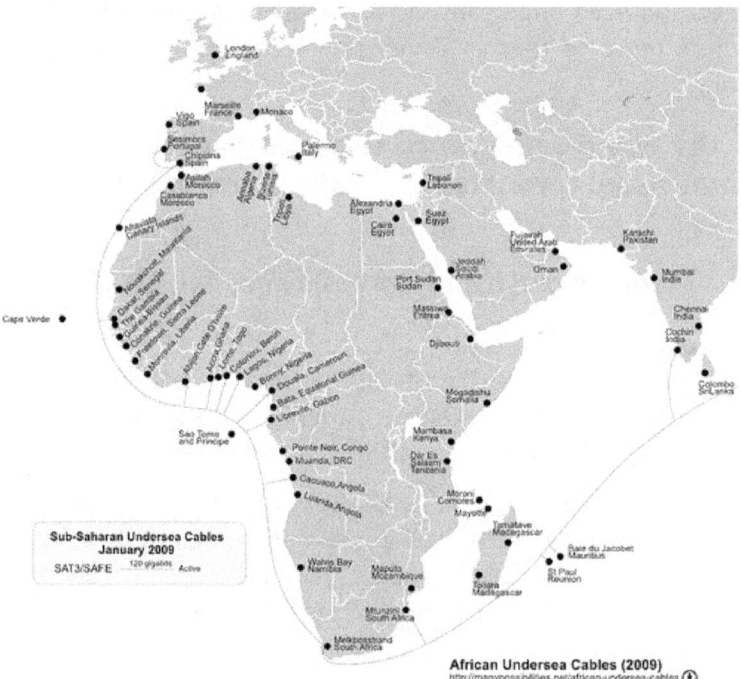

African Undersea Cables (2009)
http://manypossibilities.net/african-undersea-cables

Africa's single cable system in 2009 – manypossibilities.net

Telecoms has as its basis connectivity; the ability to connect people and devices to each other and the Internet. Above is

Dave Welmans

the single SAT-3 undersea cable that connected Africa to the rest of the world in 2009! The thickness of the lines in both graphics is relative to the carrying capacity of those cables systems.

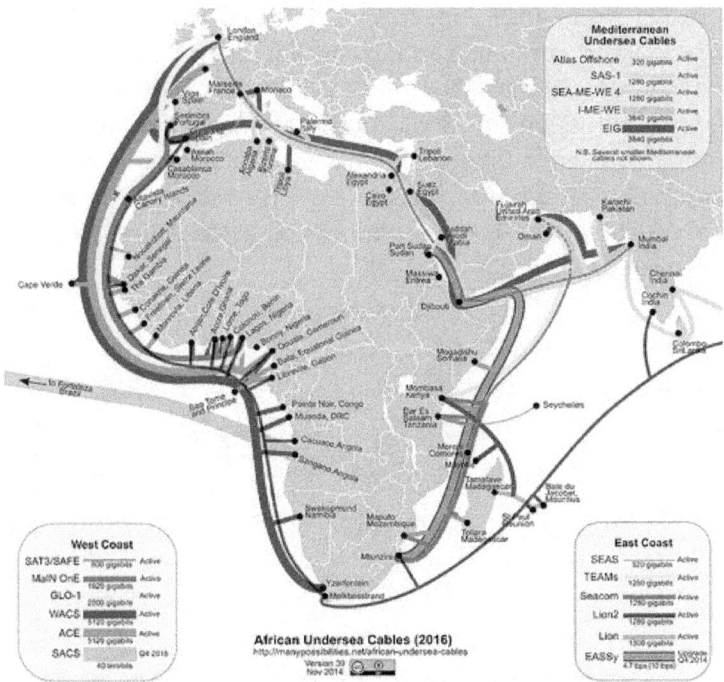

Undersea cable systems 2016 – manypossibilites.net

So Africa comes into the light in just under 7 years: an increase from 200 Gbps to 55 000 Gbps on the West coast and 13 000 Gbps on the East.

A 68 000 Gbps or a 34 000% increase over 7 years!

It is this new connectivity that forms the basis for improvements in opportunities in Africa.

Cooper's Law

Added to this quantum increase in fibre capacity around the shores of Africa is the concurrent improvement in wireless technologies.

The radio frequency spectrum is used for sending information and communications and has been doing so for over a century. When the Italian Marconi conducted his wireless transmissions in 1895, the spectrum required for the transmission used a sizable chunk of the available radio spectrum. Over a hundred years later, it is possible to send a million conversations in the same space as that first radio transmission used.

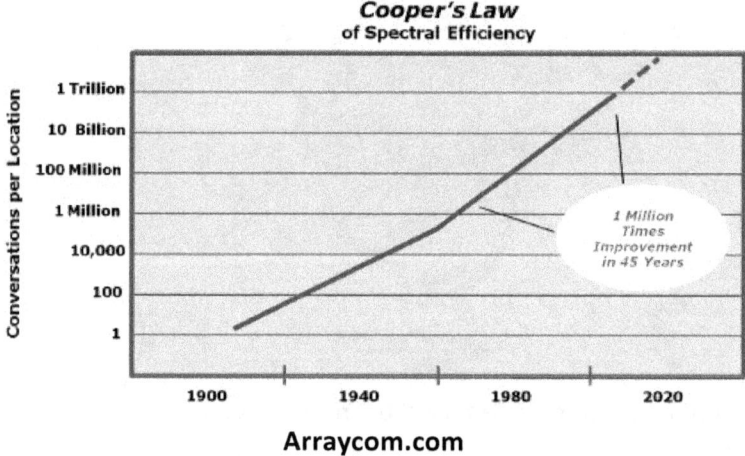

Cooper's Law
of Spectral Efficiency

Arraycom.com

Similarly to Moore's Law, this capacity follows a similar exponential growth, doubling every two-and-a-half years and it has done this for the past 104 years. Martin Cooper, Chairman Emeritus of ArrayComm, first made this observation and is dubbed "Cooper's Law." Interestingly enough he is also attributed for making the first cellular phone call while working for Motorola in 1973.

Dave Welmans

What is different to Moore's Law is that this observation could be applied going back almost 100 years showing that there has been an improvement of greater than a million times in just the last 45 years while the comparison to the initial transmission becomes a little stupid with an improvement of over a trillion times.

As the world moves into the digital age, the improvements in transistor technology described by Moore's Law also impacts on this field giving rise to further improvements.

So here we have a quantum change in fibre and wireless capacity washing up onto African shores. Africans have barely got their toes wet when we look at the technological wave and the abundant opportunities that are coming.

Connectivity in Africa

Afterfibre

The map above shows the current fibre networks in Africa and highlights the vastness that still needs to be covered.

Africa is a very large area: 31m km^2. Until recently there have been very few connections from the rest of the world to Africa and visa versa. Until 2009, there was a single undersea cable down the west coast of Africa, connecting a select few countries. Since 23 September 2009, when Seacom landed and went live on the east coast of Africa, a number of other cable systems have been completed on both the west coast and east coast of Africa bringing a total of 68 Tbps to Africa.

This new abundance of capacity has helped drive the price from around $10 000/ Mbps to <$100/Mbps.

It would appear that the lack of viable and affordable access to connectivity should have been resolved long ago. But this doesn't take into account the vastness of Africa and the additional costs to deliver this connectivity into Africa and not just some coastal towns.

First, the national backhaul carriers carry this capacity into cities and towns in Africa. The second players are those companies and institutions that spread this connectivity through a metropolitan or urban area like a spider's web.

The planning, funding and implementation of these stages takes a long time, i.e. years and not months and it is only once all these links are in place that the cost benefit can be passed on to the end users.

The high-level example of what this looks like is as follows:

- Undersea fibre cables connect Africa to other parts of the world.

Dave Welmans

- Fibre networks connect these undersea cables from their landing stations on the coast of Africa to major centres in different countries.
- The next level down is the national long-haul fibre network connecting and spreading this capacity from the major centres to each other within a country.
- After this comes the metro or urban networks that deliver this connection to larger institutions like universities, other institutions and large corporates.
- The last level is normally the service provider's network. This can be seen as your service provider's connection to your office or home. It can be in the form of copper, wireless, fibre or satellite.

The economics of deployment compounded by large distances and return on investment has prevented large-scale rollouts of fibre networks and it remains the territory of the cellular service providers to connect users to their networks and the Internet.

Voice and data

In Africa, the majority of mobile service providers had voice-centric networks but the natural evolution of these technologies will transform these networks into data networks.

Although voice connectivity and its effect have been profound and has driven the adoption of cellular technology throughout Africa, it is the addition of data connectivity that will become the major enabler for Africa.

The book's original title *The Last Billion - lighting up the Dark Continent* has particular reference to the way that new generation networks (NGN) are built on optical fibre. Networks now move information in the form of photons instead of electrical signals over copper. The increase in scalability and reduction in costs of fibre carrying capacity is the differentiating factor to copper networks. Also, the fact that copper is a sought-after commodity in Africa and is easily dug up, dragged down or carried away and converted into ready cash leads to enormous copper theft throughout Africa.

This telecoms revolution looks different to what has taken place in First World countries, where higher capacity networks are already deployed. Africa is almost skipping this stage due to the large, disparate, nature of the continent as well as the smaller revenue that can be generated out of poorer consumers and businesses with fibre.

This leads to the cellular service providers being the main providers of the last mile connection and they are becoming the *de facto* network and content providers. These providers are now in the process of upgrading their voice-centric networks to the new-generation fibre networks needed to carry the increased capacity to their towers and are deploying newer technology in the form of Long Term Evolution (LTE) technology. The increase in capacity and manageability of the spectrum in LTE networks are key for delivering higher connection rates to the end user.

Dave Welmans

Smartphone vs feature phone

The rationale for the coming digital broadband revolution prediction is the unstoppable migration from dumb phones to feature phones and finally to smartphones in Africa.

To simplify the differences:

- Dumb phone – e.g. Nokia 3310 that could make calls and send SMS'.
- Feature phone – Nokia N95 that could access the Internet, send and receive mail and do all that a dumb phone did.
- Smartphones – Apple and Samsung (including their tablets), Nokia, Blackberry. The smartphone is a good computing device. While the line between feature phones and smartphones is often blurry, access to the Internet and the ability to run apps are the features that really matter.

SMS and USSD

It is important to note the adaptability and innovation of Africans in taking the original dumb phone and adapting it to business use within Africa. Just like William Kamkwamba in the introductory chapter, Africans are masters at taking what little they have and creating new and innovative ways to use technology.

In true African fashion, much has been achieved with the dumb phone. Africans delivered the first prepaid systems, the first 'Please call me' call-backs and extensive use of USSD strings as a means of interacting with services – all on the dumb phone.

With these phones, there was no data connectivity and so the communication was limited to two types of data communication built into these devices: the USSD string and the SMS. The "Unstructured Supplementary Service Data" (USSD) is a protocol used by cellular telephones to communicate with the service provider's computers.

USSD menus can be used for browsing, prepaid call back service, mobile-money services, location-based content services, menu-based information services, and as part of configuring the phone on the network.

The USSD string is more responsive and cheaper than services that use SMS.

Service providers can use these strings as basic client menu systems. In Africa it is not uncommon for banks to have applications still running on USSD technology for their clients.

Large businesses have been created on this technology. M-Pesa, the Vodafone eWallet, and MXit, the social networking program, all created business models that took account of the end user device being a less than smart phone.

Currently it is these less than smart phones that still make up the majority of the devices in Africa although the trend is growing for people to migrate to smart phones.

The current migration creates the basis of the next wave in the telecoms revolution that has started in Africa.

The Internet wave

Fixed-line telephony and subsequently fixed-line broadband does not exist in any meaningful numbers in Africa. Even South Africa has only just reached the milestone of 1m fixed line Internet users in 2015; a mere 2% of the population, while 24m or 50% of users use mobile technology to access the Internet.

In Africa, Internet access is following the same explosive growth as that shown by mobile penetration in Africa. From an almost non-existent base of 4,5m Internet users in the whole of the continent in December 2000 the percentage of Internet users jumped to 26% or 297m users in 2014 with more than 50% of users accessing the Internet through a mobile phone.

The Internet café is being replaced by the smartphone in Africa. Initially, access for Africans was limited to Internet cafés, educational institutions and workplaces but with the cellular networks being able to carry data and the introduction of smartphones, access to the Internet has exploded.

Despite this high percentage of users using the Internet from mobile phones, the amount of usage is constrained by the cost of data through mobile networks. An increase in data capacity on the networks coupled with falling data prices will drive this growth.

Why Mobile is BIG in Africa
The newest wave, the cellular wave, has brought all of this technology flooding into the home of the average African citizen.

The device at the centre of all of this is obviously the mobile phone itself. This is augmented by the context that for many Africans this represents their first display or access device, and sometimes the *only* connection to the digital world.

The demand for low-cost phones that deliver on these features is very important. Huawei and Nokia have already built devices specifically for the African market. Africa will see a more pronounced acceleration from dumb phones and feature phones to smartphones fuelled by the use of the device as a primary Internet connection.

Running parallel to this is the link from the device to the rest of the world. Connectivity and infrastructure have seen huge investment and improvement over the last few years with undersea cables landing, coverage into more remote areas spreading, and newer technology such as Long Term Evolution (LTE) being rolled out. These two trends – demand for low-cost smartphones and investment in connectivity – will work together to drive the market with low cost, yet robust, phones that are affordable to use.

The phone as a computing device
Driven equally by Moore's Law, the improvements in the phone's computing powers will have a profound impact on our African world. Africa continues to be greatly impacted by the drop in price and increase in computing capacity of the phone.

In Africa, the need is for cheaper and more portable tablets and phones and these cheaper, portable computer-phones will be the preferred device for the African end-user compared to laptops and computers as the primary connection device around the world. This means that the phone and tablet are *the* computing devices of choice throughout Africa.

Dave Welmans

Africa had a much faster adoption rate of cellular phones than other First World countries, driven by the necessity of having the ability to phone someone anywhere in Africa. Africa doesn't have public phones on every (make that *any*) street corner. It is this latent basic need for communication and an absence of any other workable technology that drove the unprecedented, and to some, surprising, apportion of this technology in Africa.

We haven't as yet seen the same growth of feature and smartphone technologies as the dumb phone solved the primary problem of communication. The continued drop in price with increasing computing power will drive the smartphone adoption with 100m more phones being sold for every drop of $10 in price.

As networks are deployed and upgraded to handle data, in conjunction with the increased data demand we will see a natural migration of Africans to the smartphone ecosystem.

The last remaining barrier will be cost as it is always a huge factor in Africa and the availability of cheaper smartphones from Huawei and Nokia with increased processing power will eventually reach most of the continent's inhabitants.

WISPs

A smaller sector of the telecoms market has also made a hugely positive impact on delivering connectivity into rural areas. This is the space of Wireless Internet Service Providers or WISPs.

Unlicensed or public wi-fi has followed a similar explosion in technology, increasing its throughput, speed and distance. This wi-fi operates in what is called unlicensed spectrum - unlicensed in the sense that anybody with the requisite licensing can make use of this public shared spectrum. This obviates the need for costly purchasing of spectrum by the provider and allows for a lower-cost delivery of connectivity.

Think of your laptop connecting to an access point or router at home. This is normally in the 2.4 GHz wavelength or it might even be on the 5,8 GHz spectrum. It is this spectrum that is being used to deploy and extend the reach of networks within Africa.

The technology differs to mobile cellular technology in that it normally requires some form of non-mobile customer premises equipment (CPE) to capture the signal and make it available to you locally.

Although the technology for this equipment is much cheaper than cellular technology equipment the trade-off is that the spectrum is unlicensed and can quickly be over-saturated which leads to a degradation of the service.

The practical benefit for outlying and rural areas is that the capital needed to connect someone is feasible without the larger investment required of a mobile operator. There will always be a need for the WISP who is willing to connect areas that the mobile companies deem economically unfeasible.

Jenny Internet

Jenny Internet is a licensed Wireless ISP in South Africa. Enter Charles Nyezi, a rural based owner on an Internet Café in Nquthu situated in KwaZulu-Natal. This small town is a thriving industrial town strategically situated for growth in the region.

Dave Welmans

But, being such a small town means that the large telecoms operators see it as a much lesser priority to deliver services to than the metropolitan areas with higher densities. This is a common story within Africa and translates into basic lack of connectivity problems for people in Nquthu.

Prior to Jenny Internet coming to town, Charles Nyezi had the choice of dial-up connectivity at 56 kbps and with multiple days outage due to copper theft or the much more expensive but not much faster satellite connectivity. Charles chose satellite as the lesser of the two evils.

Jenny Internet brought an innovative wireless solution to Nquthu. They have a franchisee model that allows their resellers to piggyback off their core network infrastructure and ISP platform. What the franchisee needs to do is to plan to get to an interconnection point with the provider's network.

Charles needed to invest in a tower to both reach the Jenny Internet connection point as well as reach the area of coverage. They set up towers of up to 50m to do this. Once connected, Jenny Internet does all the back-end support and administration.

Werner and Rolf Stucky started Jenny Internet. They saw a gap in the market to provide services to rural and hard to reach areas throughout rural South Africa and developed their franchise model from the ground up with Rolf focussing on the marketing and business development while Werner used his German learned programming skills to create their 'Jenny Engine' from the ground up.

The cost of the tower was sponsored by a local Mercedes dealership who provided the $20 000 needed for the tower infrastructure.

The added complexity here was that in true African tradition land rights are complicated and the erection of the tower needed the support of local chiefs and councils of the Zulu owned land. Remember Shaka? Well, he could have got connected with Jenny Internet.

The choice of location and setting up of the tower was done by the two brothers and assisted by Nyezi and was erected in December 2013.

Nyezi was over the moon with the results. He now has a viable and sustainable business in rural Africa. The two biggest benefits for users are the reliability and cost of the service. The latency of the network is impressive and has been built with African conditions in mind catering for numerous electricity outages. The price that Nyezi can deliver services is approximately at a 10% cost of what was available before. The network can deliver access to thousands of people and reach 150 schools in the area as well as delivering business services to hundreds of farms and businesses.

This is an impressive tech-strat approach to fulfilling an African need for communication. The two brothers in conjunction with a local entrepreneur and in consultation with the local community have set up a thriving business and connected a small part of Africa to the rest of the world.

Dave Welmans

Data centres

A major trend in this developing market is the move away from each company investing in their own infrastructure for their data centres into using vendor-neutral data centres.

African conditions of irregular power and access to other businesses in the form of suppliers and customers can be addressed to a large extent by moving into data centres. Together with the financial savings, the data centre is an effective answer to power issues and connectivity within Africa.

Cables and wireless for Africa

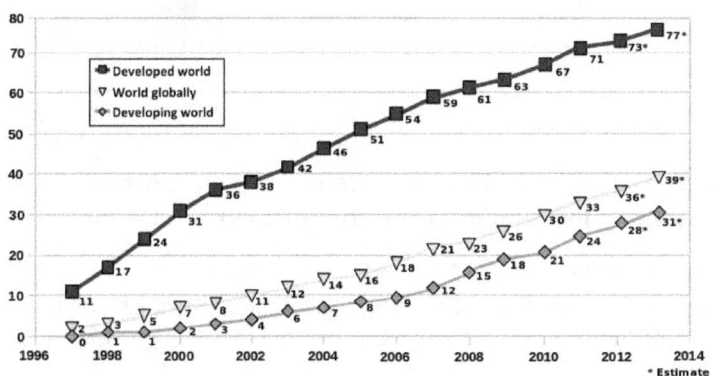

Internet users per 100 inhabitants - International Telecommunications Union

Africa is once again different to First World countries in regard to its growth in Internet users. Coming out of the 'Dark Ages' with no connectivity and moving relatively quickly into a cellular or mobile connected environment is unique and differs from countries with adequate infrastructure deployed on cable, copper and fibre connectivity.

Add to this the smartphone adoption wave starting to rise in Africa and you have a rich and potentially fertile environment in which to make great things and disrupt the status quo.

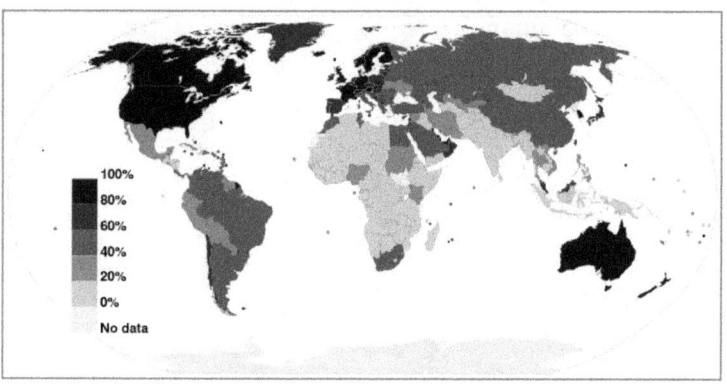

Internet users in 2012 as a percentage of a country's population - International Telecommunications Union.

Africans can now buy an Android smartphone in Kenya for less than $60. It comes with a version of Android with 5 MP camera and video capability.

For the majority of the continent, cellular or mobile is actually the only option for connectivity.

Algeria, South Africa, Gabon, Tunisia, Mauritius, Botswana, Morocco, Egypt and Mauritania all have high cellular penetration rates demonstrating that mobile connectivity is in great demand for countries that have bad fixed-line connectivity.

Dave Welmans

Current growth rates of mobile penetration means by 2020, almost every single person in Africa should own a mobile phone.

In Africa the top mobile activities for users are: Facebook, SMS, FM radio, the Internet, photos, instant messaging, Twitter and playing games.

Africa is set to become the mobile continent (no landlines, no PCs). Phones are the devices that connect African to the world and smartphones will be the computers and device of choice to connect to the Internet bringing with it changes that help economic growth and social upliftment. Once this technological revolution sweeps the whole of the continent, the exponential growth will become phenomenal.

Metcalf's Law
In telecoms and networking, there is a method of determining the value of the network by using something called Metcalf's law.

Metcalfe's law states that the value of a telecommunications network is proportional to the square of the number of connected users of the system. First observed in 1993, this law was aimed at calculating the value of other networks, specifically fax machines and landline telephones but the theory translates well for cellular networks too.

Now with the Internet being a network means that this law carries over to Internet connectivity from cellular phones in Africa. As users connect to the Internet through their phones, the telecoms network becomes exponentially valuable. Add another 300m people and the value becomes close to priceless!

FTTx

Although I have laid out the scenario of cellular operators becoming the network and content providers due to Africa's reliance on the smartphone as an access device, there is a quantum movement in urban areas for fibre to the home. (FTTH). Also known as Fibre to the Business (FTTb).

In the suburbs of Nairobi, Lagos and Johannesburg there is a drive to come up with innovative business models to get fibre connectivity to the business or home.

Developers are realising that good affordable high-speed connectivity is a fundamental component of the attractiveness of a development. It is only the archaic developer that does not work in the capital cost of installing a world-class fibre network.

The challenge has been the cost to retrofit established suburbs but even here, innovative business models are being developed that enable urban areas in African cities to become connected.

Knowledge-based societies

Alex Ntale, Atsushi Yamanaka and Didier Nkurikiyimfura relate a positive view of Rwanda's move to a knowledge-based society.

Rwanda, Africa's smallest country has recovered from its political unrest of the 1990's. Being so small also leaves Rwanda with limited resources agricultural and production resources. The Rwandan government drew up a plan to take advantage of the changes in technology that were becoming available. They created a plan called Vision 2020 that had at its core the integration technology in the form of telecoms and computers to help grow the countries economy. They developed their own 'tech-strat'.

Large-scale investment from the government and the private sector over the last few years is helping to build the necessary components needed to support this plan. The government policies also cover skills development at a school and tertiary level as well as significant investment in rolling out fibre networks is helping change this smallest of African countries. Rwanda's mobile penetration grew by over 50% in 2010 alone.

Rwanda is moving from being an agricultural economy to a knowledge-based society. This country and its progressive policies have shown that it is possible to change the previously gloomy African story from one of reliance on raw materials to one that focuses on services and development of its people.

A fresh start-up culture is growing strongly in hubs such as Nigeria, Kenya, Ghana and South Africa, with mobile devices driving this development. The African specific solutions being developed in these centres are helping to change Africa. Applications that help farmers by providing market pricing and weather reports to using cellphones to help compliance of patients to medical regimes and diagnostic tests are changing the face of Africa. The mobile revolution is being followed by the mobile Internet revolution and is having a marked change for the better in Africa by providing abundant opportunities for improvements in the way people do business.

There are some factors that are helping with this digital revolution:

- 50% of Africans are under the age of 19.

- This young demographic is not afraid of new technology. They have adopted the new digital age with alacrity.
- Most young Africans are demanding smartphones and access to networks that can support their need to become part of social networks and have access to the Internet.

Future developments

The connectivity talked about is only the basis for other services that enable communication and business. First World countries are adopting video conferencing and its big brother: tele-presence. With the deployment of higher capacity networks, business in Africa can now become meaningfully engaged with the rest of the world with these technologies.

Video communication used to be driven by proprietary software and hardware, but Skype, Facebook and Google Hangouts have all changed that.

A Google hangout can have 8 people in an interactive session while broadcasting to an unlimited number of viewers while being simultaneously recorded as a YouTube video.

Some networks in Africa have supported video calling between phones since 2010, but it was limited to people on the same network and was unreliable. Now with Facetime on iPhones, if your network is sufficiently fast, you can have a person-to-person video call across the world.

Dave Welmans

A Gmin meeting being held using Google Hangouts. Gmin is an IT idea lab based in Africa.

Here's an example of a meeting being held across continents with Google Hangouts.

In spite of their lack of office space, they've managed to execute successful projects across Sierra Leone, Kenya and South Africa.

Summary: Telecoms

Africa, and the world, has seen and felt the effect of the technological revolution brought on by the introduction of the cellphone and now stands at a point where, mostly through the success of these cellular providers and the continued evolution of cellular technology to handle data, combined with the increase in data capacity availability, Africans are about to be swept up in the next stage of this digital revolution in the form of broadband connectivity.

The combination of the exponential growth in cellular connectivity availability together with the continued migration of cellular networks to being data networks, and the increasing sophistication of the end-user access device, indicates that Africa is about to change radically.

There's a William Gibson quote that I'd like to repeat: "*the future is here, it's just not evenly distributed yet.*"

For Africa I'd interpret this as rather than waiting passively for technology to change the world, let's see how much we can do in Africa with what already exists.

- The cellular networks have laid the groundwork for new data-centric networks.
- Mobile connectivity is used by >50% of Africans to connect to the Internet.
- The drop in price and increasing power of smartphones will drive this connectivity.
- The improvements in wireless capacity are helping this mobile broadband revolution.
- Urban areas will implement FTTx while all other areas will use predominantly wireless and cellular connectivity.
- New services like video conferencing will allow Africans to join the connected First World.

Dave Welmans

10. Education

Education is one of the fields most likely to be drastically affected by this technological avalanche, both through the access to information as well as in methods of teaching.

one laptop per child

The basic requirement is for an access device and connection to stored content. The access device is required to be the capture device and display for presentation and in some cases also computation although this computation can also take place in the cloud.

OLPC

An example of what is available already in this space is the One Laptop Per Child Project (OLPC) and the Ubuntu phone software.

The Ubuntu operating system is also born out of Africa. South African IT billionaire Mark Shuttleworth developed the software.

Already the most used Linux version in schools around the world, Shuttleworth also adapted his Ubuntu Linux system to be able to run on Android phones. Loading this version of Ubuntu, called Ubuntu Edge, on the phone allows the user to use the phone as a computational device. Putting the phone in a docking station that connects to a screen for display and a keyboard and mouse for input the phone doubles up as an Ubuntu workstation.

The OLPC project has a different origin and strategy. The aim of the project was to open the development cycle for large companies to get involved in making the basic computer suitable and affordable for Third World countries.

Suitability, in this case means that it should be able to be self-powered, rugged and have a graphical interface. The development of these laptops eventually reached a cost of $209 per computer. The project only sold directly to governments and has distributed 2.4m laptops as of 2011.

The project was ground-breaking and helped pave the way for the introduction of lower cost tablets like iPads and Android tablets.

Today the cost of a tablet is cheaper than the OLPC, which means that the tablet will probably 'kill' the OLPC project.

Student-driven learning
But the results of the project have been staggering. In a moving TED talk, OLPC's founder, Nicholas Negroponte, tells the story of how they were amazed at what happened in one small village in rural Ethiopia.

10 OLPC laptops were dropped off with children that had no access to electricity or Internet connectivity. The OLPC team came back regularly to monitor progress and were amazed that the children had taught themselves how to use the device within 2 days

Dave Welmans

and managed to hack the version of Android on the computer within 6 months.

To top it all, the children in this village didn't speak English at all making this autodidactic behaviour even more impressive.

This is significant is many ways, but most importantly shows that access to technology and information is all that is required for young and enquiring minds to uplift themselves and mentor each other together to achieve amazing results.

Sugata Mitra's experiments with student-driven education show similar results from experiments in India and England. His conclusion is that children are self-learning and self-teaching where all that is required for transformative growth is access to information and some modicum of encouragement or simply permission to experiment and satisfy their curiosity.

African children are passionate about being able to go to school and learn. With the advent of the newly connected Dark Continent, these children will now have access to information on every subject. Those that have a thirst for knowledge will flourish while those children that don't will be left behind.

Broadcast and content

This access to cheap computing power combined with connectivity sets the stage for broadcasting of information and remote teaching. This means that a brilliant Canadian English teacher could allocate an hour a day to teach 10 African classrooms Shakespeare. It does limit interaction, but local mentors and facilitators can supplement this. This is one way of moving some of the intellectual wealth from around the world into African classrooms.

Online content

Go to ted.com. There is more inspirational and educational content on this single website than most people could digest in a lifetime. Last I checked it was 5 Terabytes of wonderful and inspiring stories that all children should have access to in their homes or school.

There are now many academic institutions that make school and tertiary educational content available either free or at an affordable price. MIT, Stanford, Oxford and more all make portions of their syllabi freely available online.

I've already covered in some depth the availability of cheap computing devices like the Raspberry Pi and the Arduino PLC, which will have a major impact on computer literacy in Africa. It is hoped that African children will soon be involved in creating innovative solutions for Africa.

This chapter adds another dimension to our view of Africa and its resources. The most valuable resources in Africa are not only the immense natural resources but also the potential that sits mostly untapped in the African youth.

Impossible is nothing

Ngesa Marvin, a young man from a remote village in Kenya, is a strong believer that impossible is nothing for African students.

Ngesa is a Telecommunications and information-engineering student. Being a mostly self-taught programmer, Ngesa knows the hurdles that face students in Africa. The most obvious hurdles are access to information hampered by slow and expensive Internet connections compounded by, in African terms, relatively expensive hardware. Secondly, students need an environment that provides mentorship and collaboration to help encourage them in these struggles. Ngesa encourages students to join local tech forums and communities to maximise this learning benefit for their own projects.

With unbridled enthusiasm, he is developing a computer interface to read hand gestures in the form of sign language. The programme then translates these gestures into text and audio. This application is aimed at allowing deaf and hearing-impaired people to be able to communicate more effectively.

Ngesa at the Intel XDK, 2015

"Coding can solve several problems in Africa, from unemployment & disease control, to corruption & farm automation. The boundaries are limitless; with the right education and motivation, innovations that solve today's problems will sprout from every corner of the continent,"- Ngesa Marvin, Kenya.

He bears out what has been said about access to information and the backing encouragement needed for students to persevere through the difficult times.

This story carries the theme of hope in the difference that education can make in Africa and coupled with the African approach to making the most out of what is available, something that Africans have mastered, Africans can develop localised solution for Africa.

"I believe that solutions to our daily challenges should be tailored for Africans, by Africans."

And to end the chapter a quote from Google's Larry Page for all students:

Optimism is important. You have to be a little silly about the goals you set. Have a healthy disrespect for the impossible.

Summary: Education
- Education is an area that could benefit hugely from the twin drivers of cheaper and better computing devices and increasing broadband connectivity.
- Student-driven learning is an approach that may benefit Africa.

Dave Welmans

- There is a growing ecosystem of free online content available.
- Impossible is nothing!

Dave Welmans

11. Banking

How do you deal with money in an environment where you don't have access to banks – they're a long walk and a taxi trip away if lucky – and there are only a few Automated Teller Machines (ATM's)?

Welcome to the digital age where money can be transferred with an SMS or banking app; perfect for Africa.

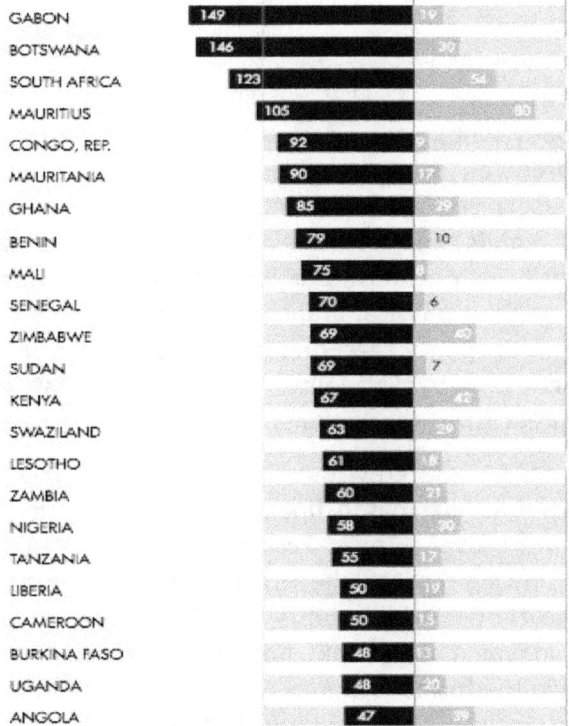

Source – APP report 2014.

Africans need to capitalise on the success of the cellular

industry. The graph shows that the cellular penetration far outstrips banking penetration. The success of this industry means that more people have phones than bank accounts. The cellular service providers have managed to reach the largely unbanked sector. This in itself creates opportunities for using the service providers as banks. These providers have historic records of cellular transactions and have a means of contacting the end user.

M-Pesa

The innovative M-Pesa service allows users to deposit money into an account stored on their  cellphones. Users can send funds to other users including suppliers of goods and services. The network provider charges a small fee for the transaction. This makes M-Pesa a virtual bank without physical branches. Their physical stores are in the form of agency agreements with networks of retail shops that act as the banks agents. Customers can draw and deposit physical cash at these points.

Once launched, M-Pesa grew quickly, and by 2010 was the most successful cellular based financial service in Africa. By 2012, there were over 17m M-Pesa accounts in Kenya and the revenue flowing through the virtual bank was pegged at $37bn or one third of the country's GDP in that year. For Africa, this means that people previously excluded from participating in the formal economy because they don't have bank accounts gain a small foothold in the financial world. The added benefit is that it also helps reduce the need for

Dave Welmans

sums of cash being carried around and this has reduced the incidence of mugging and robbery.

This has brought large sections of the population that were unbanked into the field of financial transactions using the service to send and receive money to each other as well as becoming a convenient payment system for purchases and paying bills. A rural farmer can pay for her electricity without having to do the long trip to a bank to conclude the transaction to pay the supplier.

This is one of the best examples of African tech-strat involving innovation to solve Africa specific problems. The added bonus is that, where possible, the same innovation can be exported to other Third World countries that probably have the same banking issues but also includes First World countries where the need may be different, but the innovation in the convenience may just allow the concept to become global.

M-Pesa is a virtual currency. It is backed by real money that is being paid by the person sending the money and held by the mobile service provider until withdrawn by the person receiving the money. The mobile service provider becomes a bank in effect although in reality there is strict governance surrounding the holding of the monies and management of it, but without the same constraints that exist n formal banking on both the customer and the institution.

To state the obvious, this means that your old Nokia 3310 can still send and receive payments almost anywhere. This removes the need for carrying cash and can help reduce petty crime.

As a further extension to this ecosystem, microloans can be applied for and provided through this system! Now we have a situation where someone that may be illiterate and has never been included in the formal banking sector can get access to speedy and efficient payments as well as a certain amount of credit which is better rated than other microloan companies.

Other applications can now be developed that piggyback on top of this M-Pesa ecosystem. Micro-loans and insurance are just two such examples.

Banking infrastructure

Some African banks are going digital. There are opportunities for traditional banks to be replaced by new banking institutions leveraging off strategic partnerships with other parties. An example of this is Capitec Bank in South Africa which has opened a minimum of brick and mortar branches and chooses to rely on retailers and other banking institutions infrastructure in the country.

These partnerships allow money to be deposited or withdrawn at almost any retailer in the country, which allows the bank to keep their overheads low. This lean and mean approach backed with modern technological systems allows the bank to be versatile and nimble in the marketplace bringing value to the consumer.

The bank has implemented systems like biometrics, digitised documentation and online banking allows them to compete with the traditional legacy banks.

Despite all this high-end technology, Capitec Bank also still caters for the dumb phone as well as the smart phones in South Africa. They have apps for Android and the iPhone but still make use of the USSD string technology mentioned earlier that allows dumb phones to communicate in a manner similar to instant messaging for customers to do online banking. Kudos to Capitec Bank for catering to all their mobile customers. The reliance on mobile technology applications also lowers their labour requirements, improves efficiency and productivity and makes banking available to virtually everyone.

Bitcoin and crypto-currencies

Crypto-currencies are the Pirate Bay of the financial system and Bitcoins and their block chains are the torrents of peer-to-peer financial transactions.

Bitcoin is an online payment system invented by Satoshi Nakamoto in 2008 and introduced as open-source software in 2009. Here's that open-source development approach again. It differs from M-Pesa in that there is no institution that manages the system. It uses a peer-to-peer transacting system whereby users can directly financially interact with each other without needing an intermediary. The verification and control are embedded in the publically distributed ledger called the block chain.

Being open-source means that it a currency run and developed by the masses who have an interest in using it. The currency is called a BitCoin. The system works in a totally autonomous manner without a central repository or single administrator.

Although often labelled and the first crypto-currency Bitcoin is more correctly described as the first decentralised digital currency.

Computers can be used to make or mine Bitcoins. The computing power is used to manage the 'backend' of the system, namely the ledger. This computing power is rewarded by the creation of new Bitcoins on top of transaction fees. This is known as Bitcoin mining. The Bitcoin algorithm self-manages the availability of the currency as well as the computing power to create new Bitcoins.

You don't need to have computing power to use Bitcoins as its interface to the real world is though deposits of real money, products and services.

Bitcoin as a form of payment for products and services is growing and suppliers and service providers are encouraged to accept this form of payment due to the lower transaction charges. Merchants carry the transaction fees for credit cards, while the purchaser carries this cost with Bitcoins.

The hype surrounding this currency is often linked to the encryption surrounding the transaction that can support anonymity. The block chain holds both the transaction and its value and is anonymous in the cyber world.

Understandably, established banking and financial systems have a heart attack when they can be replaced by something of this nature. No monitoring of money flows. No identification of the parties and no foreign exchange regulation. All of this means that there is no way to tax the transactions.

The Bitcoin ecosystem differs from a virtual currency, like M-Pesa, as it is not backed by real money at all but has a value as determined by the market. Think of it as a voucher that can be redeemed but the value of the voucher is determined by the demand for the voucher and how many vouchers exist: a supply and demand system that bypasses banks and international financial regulations.

Added to this, the nature of the currency makes it an international currency. This provides an insurance element for African countries that are looking to get forward cover for their own local currency while purchasing offshore.

The implication for Africa is that there are alternative financial systems that work particularly well within the digital world that they can only take advantage of these fully once they have joined the revolution.

Crowdfunding

The advent of access to the Internet will give Africans access to crowdfunding for their projects and ideas. Crowdfunding is the practice of funding a project or venture by raising monetary contributions from a large number of people, normally via the Internet.

According to Wikipedia, crowdfunding websites helped companies and individuals worldwide raise $89m in 2010, $1.47bn in 2011 and $2.66bn in 2012. In 2012 more than 1m individual campaigns were established globally and the industry was projected to grow to US $ 5.1bn in 2013.

Once Africans are online, crowdfunding opportunities will abound and can make a significant contribution to providing funding for the African start-up.

Inflows

Where international banking falls miserably short in Africa is in the field of transferring money (remittances) into Africa. These transactions are still more costly than any other region with charges that are double the world average costing Africa over $1.4bn a year more than it should.

This is not a trivial amount and in many counties in Africa this makes up more than 1% as of GDP and this amount is growing! This share of GDP is 12% for Senegal in 2010-2011.

This is a distinct disadvantage to Africa with no real substance behind the logic for this and affects many Africans repatriating money for family support and investments. It affects those most in need.

Summary: Banking

- Banking in Africa is leapfrogging more traditional banking models, mostly due to the lack of access to banks and the difficulty in transacting.
- Africa can benefit from virtual currencies that rely on mobile networks as infrastructure.
- Virtual currencies can act as an international currency, providing a means for Africa to purchase internationally
- Mobile enabled virtual currencies help include the unbanked into the economic system.
- The new connectivity allows Africans to benefit from the connected world in the form of crowdfunding.
- Remittances into Africa are more costly than any other region and double the world average.

Dave Welmans

12. Healthcare/Medicine

Africa is scary when it comes to health and healthcare. There is a plethora of exotic and deadly diseases that claims lives and affect lifestyles. Smallpox, cholera, polio, yellow fever, Dengue fever, meningitis, malaria, Dracunculiasis, Tuberculosis (TB) and Human Immunodeficiency Virus infection and acquired immune deficiency syndrome (HIV/AIDS) all take a significant toll on the populace of Africa.

Most diseases will cause severe debilitation, which limits the sufferer's ability to earn a living. Early diagnosis and cures exist for many, but diseases continue to disable and claim the lives of millions in Africa.

The tenet of this book is that a modicum of strategically delivered technology can create a huge difference. This is particularly so in the field of healthcare and medicine in Africa.

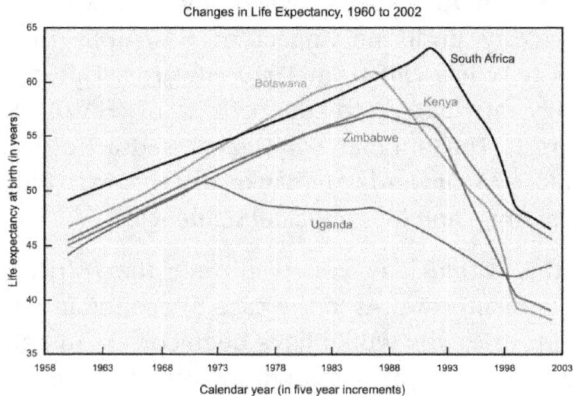

Life expectancy chart from 1958-2003 for selected countries - Wikipedia

The Last Billion

Diseases can be classified into communicable and non-communicable groups.

Medically, Africa lags far behind the whole of the rest of the world. To say that healthcare in Africa is a challenge is the understatement of the book.

An excerpt from a 2007 WHO report for Africa states:

"Health care in most of Sub-Saharan Africa remains the worst in the world. Despite decades of foreign assistance, few countries in the region are able to spend even the $34–$40 per person per year that the World Health Organization (WHO) considers the minimum necessary to provide a population with basic health care."

Not surprising when we consider the expenditure of $30-$40 per person in Africa on healthcare compared to the $8000 figure in the USA!

Life expectancy in Africa was always low but was on an upward trajectory until the impact of HIV/AIDS. The life expectancies fall off a cliff from 1980 onwards. This can be almost totally attributed to the effect of HIV/AIDS in southern Africa. The anomaly of Uganda's drastic decline from around 1973 onwards is thanks to 'The Last King of Scotland' – Idi Amin and his genocidal tendencies.

Charts like this would lead you to believe that Africa is a basket case in healthcare. As in the case of economic reform and growth in Africa you would have been correct to believe that until the first 10 years after the turn of the century. Almost all aspects of healthcare have shown great improvements. This in turn can be attributed to a change in approach to foreign funded healthcare as well as not really being able to get much worse.

Small and simple things can lead to dramatic results. Basic sanitation is often the basis of prevention of innumerable diseases. Africa can benefit from a simple improvement in living sanitisation standards that the rest of the world would consider normal.

This clearly shows why Africa lags so far behind the in healthcare as the basic level of sanitisation is at a dismal 30% compared to 90% in First World countries.

Tuberculosis, malaria, and HIV/AIDS as well as Ebola fall into the communicable diseases basket while diseases like cancer, diabetes and heart diseases fall into the non-communicable basket.

The good news is that things have taken a turn for the better over the last 10 years.

The WHO report of 2014 states: "...progress over the past decade has been remarkable."

Public healthcare is the backbone of healthcare in Africa and it is how efficiently these institutions work in conjunction with NGOs like WHO that determines the strategies required.

Communicable diseases
Communicable diseases attract world attention due to the risk of infection associated with them.

Without being too simplistic, as healthcare is not a simple landscape throughout Africa, effective remedies can be reduced to some simple strategic initiatives.

For the communicable diseases of TB, HIV/AIDS and malaria the following strategies and technologies have produced great results:

- For HIV/AIDS the current best silver bullet is prevention and for treatment the access to and consistent administering of antiretroviral treatment (ART).
- For Malaria, the single-handed campaign driven by Kingsley Holgate in the distribution of over 1m Insecticide Treated Nets (ITNs) showed how a single simple solution has effectively helped allow a greater than 50% reduction in deaths of below-five-year-olds. The Melissa and Bill Gates foundation have also done significant work in this field.
- Tuberculosis (TB) does not seem to have a silver bullet. Rather the early detection and proper consistent delivery of treatment with adherence to treatment protocols is finally having an effect. If anything, the advent of treatment-resistant TB may still undermine even these efforts.

All these technologies together with an effective strategy to deliver them throughout Africa have proven that change is possible.

Dave Welmans

HIV/AIDS in Africa

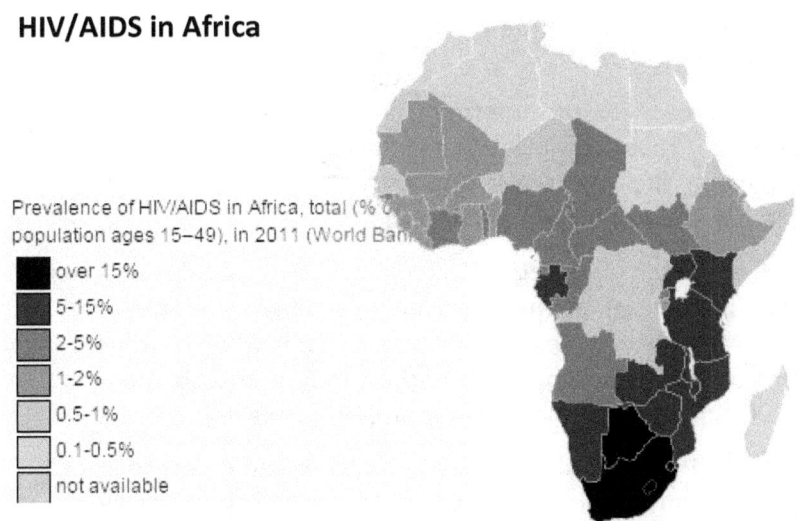

Prevalence of HIV/AIDS in Africa, total (% of population ages 15–49), in 2011 (World Bank)

- over 15%
- 5-15%
- 2-5%
- 1-2%
- 0.5-1%
- 0.1-0.5%
- not available

Although the continent is home to about 15.2% of the world's population, the shocking truth is that Sub-Saharan Africa has an estimated 69% of the HIV positive people in the world and account for 70% of all AIDS deaths in 2011.

Countries in North Africa have significantly lower infection rates, as the culture reduces the high-risk behaviours prevalent in other societies in sub-Saharan Africa.

Southern Africa is the worst affected region in Africa with more than a 10% infection rate in Botswana, Lesotho, Malawi, Mozambique, Namibia, South Africa, Swaziland, Zambia, and Zimbabwe.

A number of programs have been implemented in various parts of Africa to educate the public on HIV/AIDS. Among these are a number of prevention programmes, which is the preferred approach: the abstinence, be faithful, use a condom campaign, and the Desmond Tutu HIV Foundation's outreach programs.

The approach to the treatment and prevention of HIV has been to focus on reducing infection rates as well as expanding the coverage of Anti Retroviral Treatment (ART) to a larger and larger base of infected patients.

The advent of antiretrovirals (ARV's) and the lower-cost generic versions of these are being adopted and deployed into African countries as the primary means of treatment. This tech-strat approach of methodology and technology in the form of antiretroviral medicine (ARV) is paying off.

It should be noted here that it has taken a number of governments to decide to break the paid royalty route of proprietary ARVs and to move to purchasing cloned generics manufactured much more cheaply in places like India in an effort to be able to afford to expand the availability of these programs to achieve these results.

According to a UN organisation, UNAIDS reported in 2013 that the number of patients receiving AVR treatment by 2012 was over 700% more tan the number receiving treatment in 2005.

The number of AIDS-related deaths in sub-Saharan Africa in 2011 was a third less than the number in 2005. New HIV infections in sub-Saharan Africa in 2011 dropped by 25% compared to the infections in 2001.

This also creates a new problem: how to now deal with the surviving patients and how other diseases interact with HIV in aging populations.

There are big differences between countries in their participation in these programs. The ART coverage in

Dave Welmans

Botswana is over 95% yet a mere 38% in the Democratic Republic of Congo. The percentage of patients on ARV programs correlates to a large extent to a indication of good government for each country.

Despite these improvements, the molasses like speed of response to this crisis means that less than 7.6m of the 21m people in Africa are treated with ARV's.

Malaria
Malaria is an age old disease that has plagued many who have ventured into Africa, including Caesar, but has great impact on Africans in affected areas, which is most of Africa. In 2013, there were 200m cases of malaria reported worldwide resulting in slightly less than 600 000 deaths. Of these, more than 90% of all these deaths occur in Africa.

Of these 600 000 thousand deaths, more than 400 000 were children younger than 5 years old. It's easy to see that the young are the most at risk to die from this disease in Africa.

Malaria progress
The high malaria death rate is a disease that can best be treated by prevention. Over the first decade of the century, NGO's and governments have shown that effective remedies exist and can help reduce malaria related deaths. These interventions helped reduce deaths by more than a third in this time frame.

The better news is that the child mortality rate from malaria was reduced by 58% in the same time period.

This drastic improvement is due to the higher commitment shown by governments together with the African Union, NGO's and significantly increased international funding which saw the money spent on this disease increase form $100m in 2000 to $ 1.93bn in 2013.

There are four major interventions or tech-strategies that are proven to work.

These are:

- Availability and use of Insecticide Treated Nets (ITNs).
- Treatment with artemisinin-based combination therapies (ACT).
- Community involvement.
- Increased capacity in vector control for malaria.

As usual in Africa, the application of a technology together with an African specific methodology that involves communities, governments and NGO's working together delivers major results.

Insecticide-treated nets (ITNs)
Primarily, the education of communities together with an effective prevention strategy in the form of Insecticide treated Nets (ITNs) have helped a 31% decline in malaria incidence translating into a 49% decline in malaria deaths in the first 12 years of this decade. The funding mentioned above helped purchase and distribute ITNs either free or at a subsidised costs for affected communities.

This is a great example of when technology meets strategy delivering huge benefits.

Dave Welmans

Tuberculosis (TB)

After HIV/AIDS and malaria, Tuberculosis (TB) is the second highest killer of people worldwide due to an infectious agent and again it takes its heaviest toll in Africa.

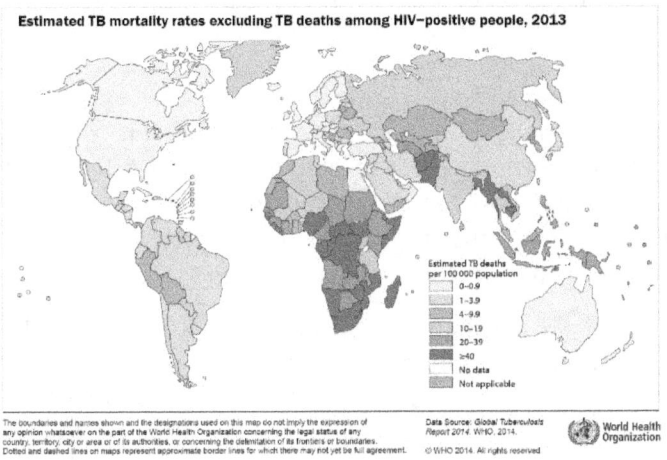

Tuberculosis (TB) is caused by the bacteria (mycobacterium tuberculosis) that mostly affects the lungs yet it is a disease that is curable and preventable.

Infection does not automatically translate into the illness. The risk is normally approximately 10% of development of the disease. The story changes when people have compromised immunity systems. People that are HIV positive, or those that suffer from malnutrition or diabetes and smokers have a much higher risk of falling ill. This shows why it affects Africa to such a large extent.

The characteristics of the disease mean that a person carrying the TB bacterium can infect up to 10-15 other people through exposure and contact per year. TB is in itself a killer and 66% of people who fall ill with TB, if untreated, will die. TB is also a leading killer of HIV-positive people causing 25% of all HIV-related deaths.

The strategy here is to focus on prevention, diagnosis and stringent treatment to be effective. Adopting this strategy has resulted in a drop of 45% in TB deaths up until 2013.

Multidrug-resistant TB
The added complication with dealing with this difficult disease is that through the use of the standard drugs over decades together with patchy enforcement of treatments, have led to TB-resistant strains. This is common throughout the world and can compromise treatment and recovery.

This strain of TB is called multidrug-resistant TB (MDR-TB). Inappropriate treatment, incorrect application of drugs as well as poor quality of drugs can all lead to drug resistant strains.

Africa still has the worst infection rates with eight of the ten countries with the highest incidence. But the slightly better news is that although the figures are still high, there has been an improvement over the last 20 years. The prevalence has dropped form 404 per 100 000 of the population to 303 per 100 0000 population in this time period.

Ebola
A disease that is top of mind in the developed world, mostly due to the nightmarish symptoms and high death rates, is Ebola. The latest outbreak in West Africa declared on 22 March 2014 in Guinea, has claimed more than 8200 lives. This is the stuff of apocalyptic nightmares. There are four affected countries in Africa: Guinea, Liberia, Sierra Leone and

Mali. Outbreaks in Nigeria and Senegal were declared over within a few weeks.

This outbreak is a classic example of Africa and the rest of the world being slow in responding to the world's 'worst health disaster'. The slow response is due to the nature of the funding of WHO. Once a crisis hits, the organisation then goes out to seek funding to get the required resources to deal with the precipitating crisis. This is a reactive and slow means of responding to any crisis.

The affected countries also fall into the category of 'weak states' that are racked with conflict and ineffective governments. The local healthcare practitioners did not have the knowledge, skills or resources to deal with the outbreak.

And as Medici Sans Frontier (MSF) reported, the initial aid from other countries focussed on financing leaving staffing up to local authorities and NGOs.

The 8 200 deaths do not reflect the extent of the problem as it had the potential of spreading across the world. The worldview that this is an African problem is short-sighted as the risk of global catastrophe trumps being able to keep an arms-length approach. The WHO announcement in August 2014 that the Ebola epidemic constituted a 'public health emergency of international concern' only led to counties essentially joining a 'global coalition of inaction'.

A better implementation of proven tech-strat methods is needed to combat this disease. Do you think the world and Africa has learned anything from this latest crisis?

Ebola in the DRC, 2014

As a case in point on how an effective tech-strat can be used to curb an outbreak is the recent outbreak in 2014 in the Democratic Republic of Congo (DRC).

There was a confirmed outbreak of Ebola in the Boende district as reported to WHO on 24 August 2014.

The DRC government and healthcare systems had dealt with 7 previous Ebola outbreaks. Due to this history, the country had the experience and skilled personnel to deal with this latest outbreak. They also had effective communication and support from WHO.

Despite being an impoverished Third World country that ranks as the poorest nation in Africa and the world, experience had taught them how to deal effectively with this outbreak.

The effort was not only supported but also personally supervised by the president. The response team set up a national committee that met daily in Kinshasa to strategize and track the progress being made. The experienced healthcare professionals included specialists that had been involved in previous outbreaks.

Classical control measures to detect, isolate, and prevent further infection were used to quickly control the outbreak. The government also placed some areas under quarantine to limit further population movement and risk.

This outbreak was confirmed over with the last case being reported on 4 October 2014. This shows that even the poorest country in the world can deal effectively with health crisis like Ebola.

Dave Welmans

Here in Africa, both TB and Ebola can be managed by an effective tech-strat approach. What is key is knowledge and training to be able to deal with these epidemics.

Non-communicable diseases

"Non-communicable diseases are on the rise in the African region. At the same time, we face the unfinished business of major communicable diseases and maternal and child health problems."
Sambo, March 2013.

Although these communicable diseases grab the lion's share of press coverage, non-communicable diseases are starting to affect African lifestyles as Africans adopt more westernised lifestyles.

As with the technological surge throughout Africa over the last decade, the prevalence of NCD's on the continent is also on the increase. Diseases and causes of death that are most common in First World countries are becoming healthcare burdens in Africa: cardiovascular disease, diabetes, cancer, chronic respiratory illnesses like asthma are taking hold in African lives. Death by violence and road accidents are on the increase. This affects the population group of those above 45 most and the statistics show that 62% of Africans now die from NCDs.

This change can be attributed to the 'benefits' of westernisation with changes in diets and lifestyles that leave Africans following the path of First World countries in regard to NCDs.

eHealth

eHealth solutions are an example of using technology in new and innovative ways to deliver on health solutions in Africa. Digitisation and connectivity can provide health workers with secure access to patient information with tools like electronic medical records to provide better health care. This is perfect for Africa with patients in rural areas as it helps eliminate the need to spend money on travelling to a clinic where cellphones can be used to contact health workers that then have access to patient information and medical records stored electronically and can dispense advice before incurring the cost and effort needed to visit the clinic.

"It also demonstrated how using innovative eLearning tools could reach remote areas and narrow the usual knowledge and access gap between rural and urban districts."
A Decade of WHO in the African region.

Summary: Healthcare

In summary of this chapter, it is clear that there are African solutions to some of the biggest healthcare challenges in Africa. The execution of these strategies will determine how quickly Africa can move out of their Third World healthcare status.

- Communicable diseases still dominate the healthcare budget in Africa.
- Effective strategies together with new technology in the form of ARVs and ITNs are having a positive effect in Africa.
- Quick and effective management can handle Ebola.

Dave Welmans

To end on a positive note, following is a graph on Maternal Mortality Rates worldwide. Africa is predictably on the wrong end of the graph again but is a region showing great improvement.

Fig. 1.2. **Maternal mortality ratio (per 100 000 live births) by WHO region, 1990–2013**

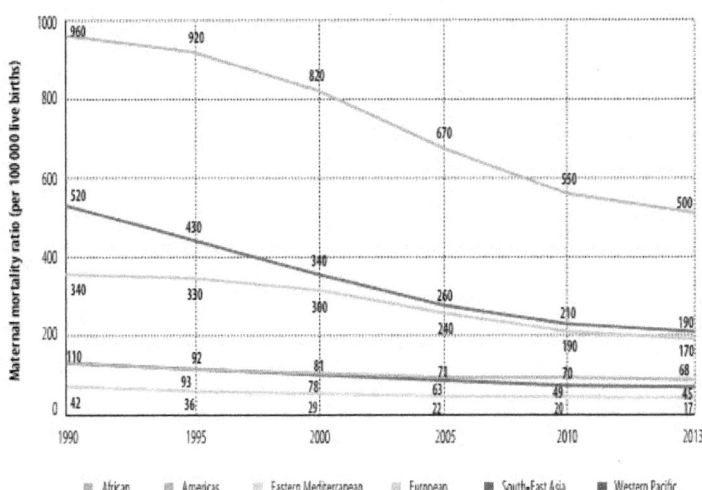

Source: adapted from World health statistics 2014. Geneva: World Health Organization; 2014.

The Last Billion

Dave Welmans

13. Energy

Energy must be the single biggest obstacle to growth in Africa and, as you shall see, the current opportunity for Africa could be to determine a new approach as to how the world produces and distributes energy, turning energy into Africa's biggest opportunity.

It has been suggested that another way of determining First or Third World status could be based on access to cost-effective and reliable energy. Anyone that has travelled in Africa will know that a constant electricity supply is rare and more than two-thirds of the population do not have access to electricity at all.

Africa has the opportunity to change the traditional fossil fuel approach that has been implemented in other regions and leapfrog the clever use of technology to help accelerate growth.

The Africa Progress Panel (APP) and their 2015 report from which I have drawn heavily, as I am not a specialist in energy, consists of 10 distinguished individuals from the private and public sector who advocate for equitable and sustainable development for Africa. Mr. Kofi Annan is the chairman of the APP. As a former secretary-general of the United Nations and Nobel laureate he brings a wealth of value to the panel. Other distinguished members include Graca Machel and Sir Bob Geldof of Band-Aid fame.

These high-profile dignitaries bring their experience and African-specific knowledge to bear in mostly an advisory role informing Africans and the world of the state of affairs in Africa. They have an unprecedented capability to interact in the worlds of business, diplomacy and politics across the world. Their insight and research provide input into their annual reports focusing on a specific sector per year giving realistic views of the problems and potential opportunities and solutions within Africa.

In their own words:

"The panel builds coalitions to leverage and broker knowledge and to convene decision-makers to create change in Africa. The panel has extensive networks of policy analysts and think tanks across Africa and the world. By bringing together the latest thinking from these knowledge and political networks, the APP contributes to generating evidence-based policies that can drive the transformation of the continent."

The latest report in 2015 focuses primarily on the problems and opportunities in the field of energy and climate change in Africa. In this report, the panel looks at the need for power and particularly alternative and sustainable power. They draw the link from traditional energy production to global warming and suggest that Africa can be a global game-changer in the field of energy production in the coming decades.

**"Can the world prevent catastrophic climate change while building the energy systems needed to sustain growth, create jobs and lift millions of people out of poverty? That question goes to the heart of the defining development challenges of the 21st century."
The APP report, 2015.**

Dave Welmans

The current crisis

The panel notes that energy use and current development varies widely across Africa, with some countries being in a position to export energy to neighbours while yet others lack even the most basic of infrastructures to generate energy.

From the viewpoint of the World Bank 25 of the 54 nations in Africa are in an energy crisis.

Africa's energy capacity has not kept pace with the rising demand for energy in the developing regions. This economic growth has placed an inordinate strain on Africa's existing resources in the first two decades of the 21st century. GDP has outstripped the growth in energy production capability. Half of the African countries grew by over 4.5% but energy generation capacity only grew by 1.2%

Despite being rich in energy resources, Africa is still lacking in energy supply. Reliable and cost-effective access to electricity is the basis for growth in a region that accounts for 15% of the world's population but only 4% of its energy demand.

More than 620m people in Africa still live without access to electricity while nearly 730m people use hazardous, inefficient forms of cooking.

The International Energy Agency's Africa Energy Outlook, 2014

To put this in perspective, Spain uses more energy than the whole of sub-Saharan Africa excluding South Africa. To compound the problem, the fuelwood (mainly charcoal) being used for cooking and lighting is degrading the environment at an alarming rate and creating a myriad of pollution-based diseases.

The use of this charcoal and the subsequent health impact is considerable. The use of this solid biomass is prevalent throughout Africa and 4 out of 5 families rely on it in their homes. The health impact is that 600 000 people die in Africa from this pollution. Half of this number is made up of children under the age of 5.

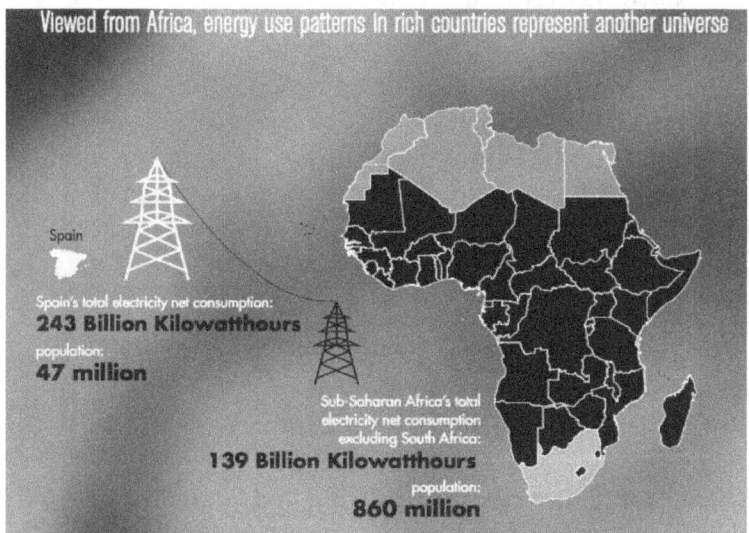

Source – The APP report 2015

In their report on this energy situation in Africa, the 2015 APP report also strongly recommends that Africa not follow the rest of the industrialised world into fossil fuel energy production and chose a different path that can help mitigate the effects of climate change.

Dave Welmans

"Climate change demands that we rethink the relationship between energy and development. The carbon-intensive energy systems that drive our economies have set us on a collision course with our planetary boundaries."

The APP report, 2015

Africa is in a unique position to choose a different path in this industrialisation. This collision between demand for energy and the climate affecting fuel burning can be avoided, as the technology, ingenuity and finance exist to make this dream a reality. Much has been said about this but the African countries still display a lack of willingness to implement this. There are a number of major summits planned for 2015 on finance and the sustainable development goals as well as climate change and they will all provide an opportunity to start this process.

Underdeveloped and developing countries in Africa are uniquely positioned to be part of the alternative energy that creates this new energy Utopia. This is a situation where African countries can lead the world in low-carbon, climate resilient energy development. The application of these new energy technologies, if executed correctly, can expand its power generation capacity and achieve universal access to energy for its people and in so doing leapfrog other countries in the development and use of alternative energy systems across the world.

This is not a solution that is for the benefit of Africa alone, but can translate into a huge gain for the world in avoiding the high-carbon route followed by today's rich world and emerging markets.

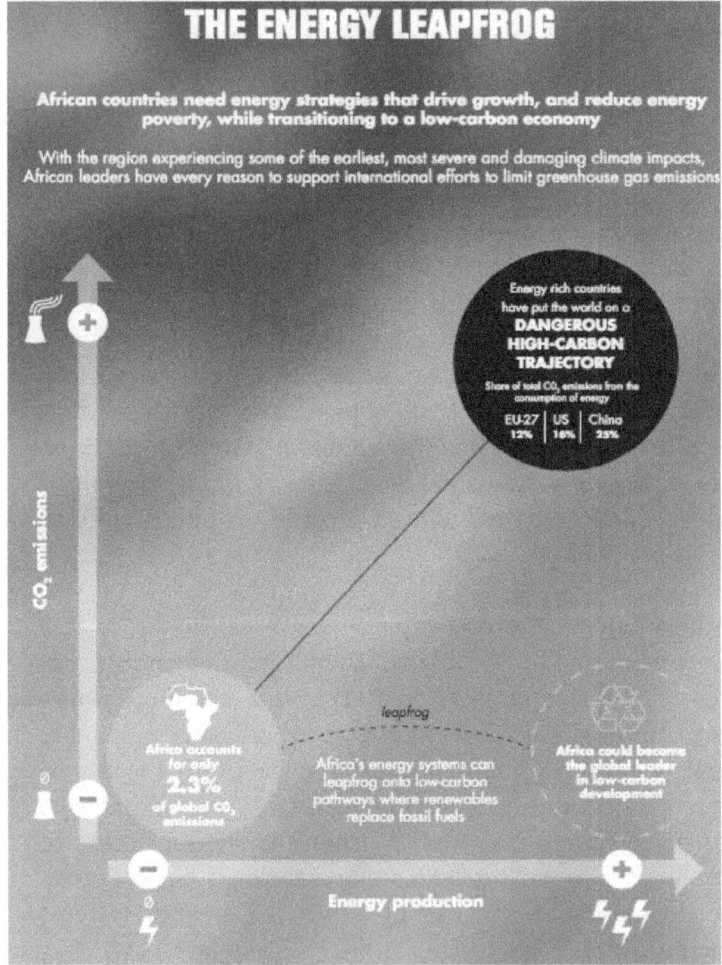

App report, 2015

Dave Welmans

"Africa has enormous potential for cleaner energy – natural gas and hydro, solar, wind and geothermal power - and should seek ways to move past the damaging energy systems that have brought the world to the brink of catastrophe."

The APP report, 2015

The fallout from standard fossil-based energy production has resulted in climate change that affects the whole world. The opportunity is for low-carbon energy production. The governments of the world need to sever the link between economic growth and greenhouse gas emissions. The alternative energy systems of natural gas, solar power, geothermal and wind energy are all within grasp. At the same time, these alternative energy systems need to help support economic growth and job creation within Africa.

The challenge

Despite the potential for an energy Utopia in Africa, the current situation is as far from the goal as can be imagined.

The amount of money being spent by the some of the world's poorest people is draining the ability of normal households to escape poverty. The current energy situation is a dismal failure. The statistics show that 138m households comprising people living on less than $2.50 per day are spending a disproportionate amount on energy, mostly in the form of charcoal, candles and paraffin. This spend is close to $10bn annually.

These new energy systems envisaged will help create investment opportunities while at the same time reducing poverty by increasing household savings.

These poorest of households spend 20 times the amount spent by First World households that are on the grid.

The challenge is to increase Africa's energy production while at the same time not having a further adverse effect on the already fragile world climate.

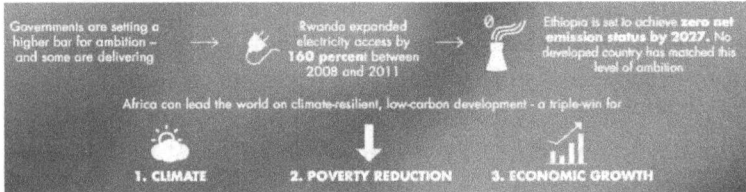

The innovation in alternative energy and low-carbon production can help deal with this concern over the impact on the world climate giving impetus to potentially new solutions in energy production.

The problem

Access to electricity and the infrastructure necessary to generate and deliver this is critical for economic development in Africa. This infrastructure is severely lacking. Only a small percentage of Africans are connected to a grid and the supply of electricity is often unreliable necessitating the use of generators that are costly to run. The cost of electricity in Africa is also amongst the highest in the world

Dave Welmans

and losses due to poorly maintained infrastructure networks are twice as high as the world average.

This lack of reliable electricity supply is identified by enterprises as the biggest hurdle to growth of business in Africa, trumping access to finance and corruption.

There are programs in Africa aimed at reversing this problem. Africa is raising capital and investing this in new generation capacity. The APP predicts that the generating capacity can quadruple by the year 2040. This is from the very low base of 90 GW today; half of half comes out of South Africa.

The areas to benefit most from this will be the urban areas whereas the rest can benefit from mini-grid and off-grid systems.

This investment will result in modern and more efficient power systems that are more efficient and will bring access to a larger portion of the poorest in Africa.

The International Energy Agency (IEA) report on African energy finds that increasing access to reliable, modern energy can turbo-charge economic growth in sub-Saharan Africa. Africa has sufficient resources to generate the needed energy but these resources are unevenly dis   tributed.
Regional integration will go some way towards addressing this problem.

The problem with biomass
The traditional energy source in Africa is still biomass in the form of charcoal and wood, the use of which is severely damaging the environment and causing destruction of the landscape. This use of charcoal and wood for energy is still

prevalent if Africa with 86% of people in Sub-Saharan Africa relying on it in some form for cooking or heating.

As in all the previous chapters, there is a change happening in Africa and the momentum for change in energy production is real with the UN program on sustainable energy being a part of this.

There is a strong push by global institutions to create an energy revolution, with sub-Saharan Africa as the centre of attention.

McKinsey Brighter Africa Report, 2015

The McKingsey Brighter Africa report of 2015 notes that if renewable energy becomes the focus of energy production, Africa could reach a 27% reduction in carbon emissions.

Renewable energy

There is a focus on renewable energy technology in Africa. There are numerous small-scale solar, wind and geothermal projects producing power for both urban and rural populations.

These projects are often best suited in remote locations as it helps deal with the problem of power distribution from large power utilities to these regions.

The potential of renewable energy is such that in itself it could alleviate much of the energy problems that Africans face every day, especially so if it can be done in a sustainable manner.

The access to energy is fundamental and essential to help reduce poverty and promote growth. The digital world outlined earlier and the telecommunication equipment necessary for the coming revolution, as well as all the other sectors including education, farming, basic industrialisation, all require reliable, and cost-effective energy access.

Renewable energy is by definition clean and free and if deployed will help protect the environment from further destruction, while providing the necessary energy for economic growth. There are a number of major sources of renewable energy that are available today.

Solar power
Africa straddles the equator and has abundant sunlight of a quality much brighter than that which Europe receives. The quality of sunlight throughout Africa is such that over 85% of Africa receives in excess of 2000 kWh/m² a year. To put this in perspective, a solar generating facility built in North Africa and comprising of just 0.3% of this area would be able to generate enough energy to supply the whole of the European Union.

This abundant supply of sunlight throughout Africa makes solar energy one of the best options to deliver energy to almost any location in Africa and in so doing can also reduce the need for large-scale infrastructure deployments to distribute conventionally produced energy.

There are a number of large-scale solar energy-generating facilities under development in Africa including projects in South Africa on the southern tip and Algeria in the north.

The real potential of solar, however, may be to provide smaller scale energy production in a distributed manner as well as on a household level. This energy could be used to help with normal everyday needs such as household electrification, water pumping, and water purification.

One large-scale project is the 8.5MW solar farm at Agahozo-Shalom Youth Village, in the eastern province of Rwanda. The plant consists of 28 360 photovoltaic panels and now produces as much as 6% of the Rwandan total electrical supply. This project was funded and built in conjunction with US, Israeli, Dutch, Norwegian, Finnish and UK backing and expertise.

On a smaller scale, there are a number of other grid-linked power utilities, including the 250 kW Kigali Solaire solar power station in Rwanda. The South Africa Renewable Energy Independent Power Producer Procurement Program has developed several projects including the Jasper Solar Energy Project (96MW), the Lesedi PV project (75MW), and the Letsatsi PV Project (75MW), which were all built by the American company SolarReserve and went live in 2014.

Power Up Gambia in a non-profit organisation operating in The Gambia. They have deployed solar power systems to healthcare facilities in Gambia in order to provide a reliable source of electricity for critical medical facilities including lighting, diagnostic testing, treatments, and water pumping. In West Africa, Energy For Opportunity (EFO), a non-profit organisation, have deployed solar power systems in schools and health care clinics as well setting up community charging stations. They also run classes to teach students photovoltaic installations at local institutions.

Dave Welmans

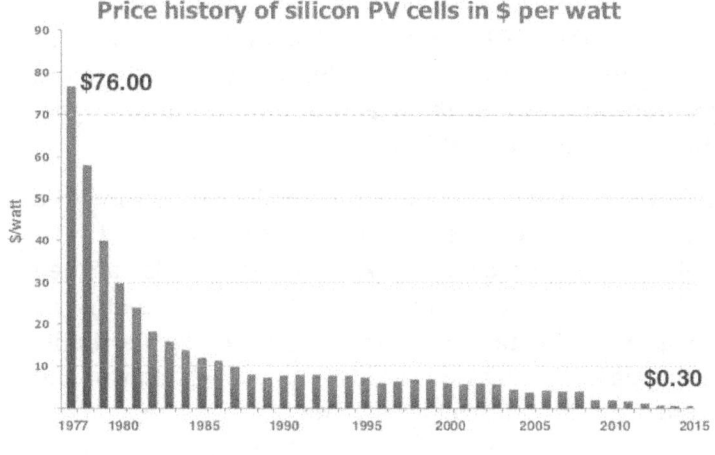

Source: Bloomberg, New Energy Finance & pv.energytrend.com

Source – Bloomberg, New Energy Finance, et al.

There are a number of plans to build large-scale solar farms in North Africa taking advantage of the deserts to supply power for Europe. Two of these projects are the Desertec project and the TuNur project. The first is funded and backed by European companies and aims to supply it via a high-voltage network to Europe as well as some local countries. The size of this project may eventually supply up to 15% of continental Europe's electricity. The second project, based in Tunisia, will be able to supply up to 3GW of power for the UK.

Part of this renewable energy revolution is the continuing drop in the price of the photovoltaic (PV) cells. The price of PV has dropped for $76 per watt generated in 1997 to around $0.30 in 2015. This price reduction is making it cost-effective to deploy and in all a better investment that traditional fossil-fuelled plants.

Grid-parity is when the price of alternative energy production is similar to the retail price of traditionally generated electricity. The cost for PV is within this bracket and there are a number of efficiencies that can be implemented to gain even further benefit form this technology source.

PV works on turning light energy into an electric current. The efficiency of this has a great impact on energy output. The relatively simple process of keeping the cells aligned optimally to the sun can increase efficiency by up to 50%. As described in the Digital Revolution chapter earlier, a simple computing device such as the Arduino with a light sensor and motors to align the cells will achieve this.

Wave and wind resources

I've beaten you over the head with how huge Africa and yet Africa's coastline is only moderate considering the land area. Moderate as it only stretches 26 000km (16 000mi) because it does not have all the indentations prevalent in a lot of European countries, but 26 000km is still pretty long. A long coastline provides opportunity for wind and wave generated energy.

There are downsides to wind energy, though. It is not as evenly distributed throughout Africa and to be harnessed on a large scale, specific location characteristics must be in place: special topographical funnelling features normally found near the coast and mountain ranges. These sites exist in north and south of the continent. The West coast of Africa is well suited to this type of energy production. The potential for energy production here is substantial, exceeding 3750 kWh.

Dave Welmans

Geothermal resources

The Great Rift Valley in the eastern part of Africa sits on top of most of this potential thermal power, but there are many other locations of high geothermal potential throughout Africa. The Great Rift Valley stretches for almost 6000km or 3700 miles in length and spans several countries in East Africa including Eritrea, Ethiopia, Djibouti, Kenya, Uganda, and Zambia.

Is nuclear in Africa's future?

The only country with aspirations to develop nuclear energy is South Africa that already has nearly two gigawatts in nuclear capacity. They have signed memorandums of understanding to co-operate on developing further nuclear energy with China, France, Japan, Russia, South Korea, and the United States, and have just recently signed a 20 year agreement with Russia to help develop up to 6 more nuclear power plants. Nuclear energy is widely regarded as a more expensive source than other available options.

Shale gas

Shale gas has proven to be the new Utopia/dystopia for energy worldwide and Africa has reserves for shale gas across sub-Saharan Africa estimated to be 4000bn cubic meters, with 52% of this amount from South Africa and 35% from Mauritania.

The effect of this shale gas on the power markets has already been made abundantly clear, but its viability will depend on the location of the gas site and cost of production. Shale gas in South Africa will potentially have the biggest effect on the markets as it has the ability to displace coal-fired power stations that exist in South Africa. At least the shale gas refining will result in significant decrease in carbon emissions.

Rwanda leads the way again

Once again, the strategy of the Rwandan government to promote local development backed by supporting policies has helped transform the energy front in that country.

As recently as 2008, Rwanda only supplied electricity to 6% of its 10m population. Those lucky enough to have access still suffered frequent power cuts. The impact of this lack of reliable energy affected business and even education. The unreliability led the school to suspend computer-learning programs. Their biggest industries of coffee and tea production lagged far below optimum capacity. The high fuel costs for back-up generators eroded business incomes.

This story has changed dramatically over the last few years. By 2012 the government of Rwanda together with the World Bank changed the energy outlook for the majority of people in the country for the better.

The World Bank and Rwandan government's strategy was to support key transformational projects to achieve maximum change.

Lucio Monari, sector manager for the bank's Africa Energy program:

"The Rwanda Electricity Rollout Program has helped to triple connections in just three years — a large outcome by any measure, and our Rwandan partners have reason to be proud of this achievement."

Dave Welmans

This increase in access, cost and reliability has paid great dividends for the countries economy benefiting normal households, small and large businesses. The reliability and cost reduction are the largest factors translating into better production and thereby competitiveness for small business as well as the major tea industry leading to better profits, sustainability and more jobs in the industry.

For locals, the benefit is having light after dark and – as in the first chapter – being able to charge their cellphones!

The technological impact here is on two fronts: both the lighting and heating technology is making an impact, but the means of managing, distributing and paying for these technologies is tightly integrated into the cellular payment systems. This comes back to a very good example of how other systems and sectors can piggyback on top of the successful mobile operators to benefit their own businesses. The payment mechanism, as well as the pre-paid vouchers makes use of the cellular companies technology.

This integration means that telecoms and cellular technology is providing both the banking payment system for people that do not have bank accounts as well as delivering the vouchers to people that don't have other means of communication with the government. This is the clever tech-strat that works in Africa. Not only a single industry but also the ancillary support provided by this technology is what makes this work.

Summary: Energy
Energy is the lifeblood of industry and forms the basis for a better quality of life. The choice of an effective tech-strat by the governments, NGOs and private enterprises is at the

heart of being able to unlock the energy potential, which is essential for all other industries, within Africa.

Africa has the opportunity of not following the traditional industrialised nations development path but can strategically choose their own energy development path.

Africa has the choice to produce and use electricity in a manner that differs from the rest of the world. They can choose to augment their energy needs with all the alternative energy supplies mentioned above.

- Energy is a huge constraint on African growth.
- If resolved, universal energy access could "turbo-charge" African economies.
- Other than the telecoms revolution, this is the largest factor that can benefit Africa.

On a small scale, households do not need to be totally driven by electricity but can combine these alternative forms of energy to deliver a better long-term result. Heat exchange systems, solar energy converted to electricity through photovoltaic and gas from bio-waste for lighting and cooking can all contribute to a more efficient energy footprint.

The time is ripe for these technologies to start making a difference for Africa.

In the next chapter, I examine a number of technologies that have the potential of disrupting business in Africa.

14.Future technological disruptors

Looking ahead, I see five spheres in technology and business that are set to disrupt the status quo in Africa:

- Telecoms
- Energy
- Transport and drones
- 3-D printing
- Industry

Telecoms

The book has focussed extensively on computer technology and telecoms and its subsequent impact on Africa. I believe that this is only the beginning of the telecoms revolution for Africa. The greatest challenges that remain are still the vast distances and subsequent cost to connect people at the bottom of the African pyramid.

Within telecoms there are a number of projects that are set to change Internet availability if or when they reach maturity.

SKA

The deployment of the Square Kilometre Array (SKA) and its tremendous bandwidth requirements is going to make the current bandwidth available in Africa pale in comparison over the next decade.

The SKA is a large-scale telescope and its size will make it 50 times more sensitive than any other radio instrument that exists today. It will require very high-performance central computing power (which will mostly reside in Europe) and long-haul links with a capacity that exceeds the current global Internet traffic.

This bandwidth hungry application with high-end computing power will be able to survey the sky more than ten thousand times faster than ever before.

The SKA project offers an environment in which governments, industry and research organisations can work together in a global partnership with a mutually beneficial common goal.

Wordlesstech.com

For this ultra-sensitive telescope to work, areas had to be chosen that were isolated from man-made 'noise' and is the reason for Australia and Africa being chosen for this deployment.

The quantum leap necessary for this project requires ground breaking technology to support it and can be likened to the American Apollo missions of the 1960's. The final deployment is years away but the initial upfront benefit will be the additional increase in low latency fibre capacity and connectivity from Africa to Europe and Australia. Although I've covered the growth in capacity linking Africa to Europe, the cabling systems have mostly connected Africa to Europe. These super highways have not connected Africa to Australia, but this project will certainly help transform this sector of

Dave Welmans

telecoms as the bandwidth requirement is estimated at more than double the current planned cable system capacity that exists.

Other than being able to find extra-terrestrials and seeing as far back as the Big Bang other connectivity projects are afoot that promise wider and more connectivity.

The Last Billion – us in Africa – will eventually become meaningfully connected to the rest of the world. There are a number of initiatives that I believe will change the landscape.

Google is a player in this connectivity space with two irons in the fire: the Google X Loon project as well as investing in the Low Earth Orbit satellite project of Elon Musk and his SpaceX company.

Facebook has also recently announced a high-altitude unmanned solar-powered plane to bring Facebook and the Internet to underserviced areas. All these projects are geared at reaching the unreachable which is an apt description for the Dark Continent.

Project Loon
As Google says on their Project Loon page: many of us think of the Internet as a global community, but two-thirds of the world's population does not yet have Internet access. Their Project Loon is aimed at addressing this problem.

Project Loon is a network of balloons traveling twice as high as commercial aircraft fly, designed to help connect people in rural and remote areas (remember that 70% of Africans still live in rural areas), help fill coverage gaps and bring people back online after disasters.

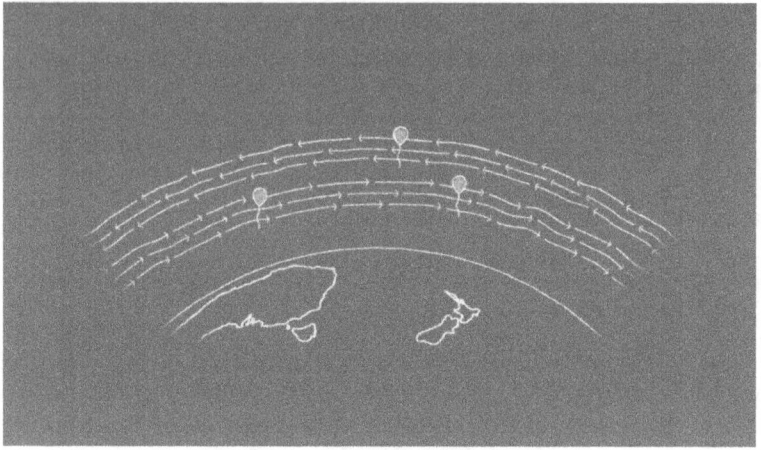

Source – designboom.com

The Loon balloons will float 20km above the Earth's surface in the stratosphere. Here, the winds are stratified, meaning that they create layers where each layer of wind varies in speed and direction. The technology supplied by Google uses software algorithms to determine where its balloons need to go and then using small on-board motors, move the balloon into a layer of wind blowing in the right direction. This complex positioning allows Google to create one large communications network.

Each balloon can provide connectivity to a ground area about 40km in diameter using a wireless communications technology called Long Term Evolution (LTE). In order to be able to use this cellular technology, Google will partner with local telecommunications companies in order to use their licensed cellular spectrum. This will enable people to access the Internet everywhere directly from their phones and other LTE-enabled devices. These balloons in turn, relay network traffic from cell phones and other devices back to the global Internet using high-speed links.

Dave Welmans

Low Earth Orbit Satellites (LEOS)

Elon Musk is known for his entrepreneurial endeavours from cyber companies like Zip2 and Paypal, electric car manufacturer Tesla and his aerospace company SpaceX. They all have as their basis new ways of applying either new or re-engineered technology solutions. He aims at large endeavours that other companies may shy away from, so when he decides to combine two areas of his experience where he has already made significant game-changing headway, the world takes notice.

The *Wall Street Journal* (WSJ) recently reported that he would be combining his expertise in satellites (SpaceX) and the cyberworld (Paypal and Zip2) in a new initiative aimed at expanding Internet connectivity to hard to reach places through a deployment of Low Earth Orbit Satellites (LEOS). As is his trademark, he breaks the mould of conventional business models and is now exploring ways to develop smaller, less expensive satellites that can deliver global Internet access. Elon Musk has confirmed that his company SpaceX is developing new advanced "micro-satellites" to deliver Internet connectivity.

The idea to deliver Internet connectivity and telecoms communication from satellites is not new and a number of companies have failed at this over the last decade or so. What Musk is doing is bringing the best technology available from other industries in a new business model to deliver this solution.

Satellites are expensive to develop, build and launch but he is focussing on micro-satellites that will be cheaper and easier to launch together with sophisticated software, similar to the Google Loon balloon project, to create a telecoms network in the sky.

He is avoiding the high altitude geostationary route as this is firstly expensive and secondly introduces an added problem of latency that is needed for communication to reach these devices and return. Finally, the devices on the ground need to be more powerful to connect to these satellites.

The smaller LEOS travel at only a third of the distance from the earth of traditional satellites solving the first three problems but introducing a new hurdle for this design. These LEOS are much closer to earth and therefore cover a much smaller area. To create meaningful coverage a network of satellites will have to be deployed.

This is where sophisticated software is needed to manage connectivity and hand-off between satellites. Luckily, this is something that cellular networks are good at and this is basically a telecoms network with each satellite being the equivalent of a tower.

Musk has called on experts in these fields to collaborate on this project. Greg Wyler, a satellite-industry veteran and former Google executive has been co-opted for this project. Wyler founded WorldVu Satellites and Musk also has Google funding to back the project. Google have reportedly promised up to $1bn in funding for this project.

Musk and Wyler have said that they'd need up to 4000 satellites for the network. These satellites will weigh 100kg (250 pounds) or about half the current smallest communication satellite. When launched, this network would be 10 times the size of the largest satellite communication's fleet, currently managed by Iridium Communications.

The benefit of the network is that it would speed up the flow of data on the Internet and deliver cost-effective, high-speed

Dave Welmans

Internet to the three billion-plus people who still have poor access – 1 billion in Africa.

Facebook's drones

One of the other big boys in cyberspace is Facebook and Mark Zuckerberg is developing solar-powered drones to provide connectivity to billions of people currently without access. Facebook's Connectivity Labs is where this project is housed and together with partnerships from Inernet.org is looking to deploy an early version of this network into Ghana, Tanzania, Kenya, Zambia and Columbia.

Connecting the World from the Sky

Facebook drone concept - Facebook

The approach is similar to project Loon and the SpaceX inintiative and aims to deliver connectivity by building a telecoms network in the sky. This time the carrier will be unmanned solar powered drones that can stay up in the air for extended periods of time. They aim to fly at about the same height as the Google Loon balloons.

So here we have Google with two projects, SpaceX and Facebook all vying to deliver connectivity to the dark spots on the globe. These three projects are not the only projects on the go but I thought we'd stick to the most visible and historically successful telecoms game-changers.

These projects have the ability to be serious disruptors to the status quo for cellular operators on the continent, but I'd imagine that some form of partnership would be entered into with the local, and literally, on-the-ground service providers collecting the money and providing ancillary services.

Energy
Energy production and distribution of this energy over large distances are two of the constraints on universal energy access in Africa. Storage of this regularly generated electricity or alternative forms like solar and wind power are critical to Africa. Batteries are the simple answer.

Tesla Giga Battery Factory
Elon Musk, the same as just mentioned in the LEOS project, is building the world's biggest battery factory. It will focus on lithium-ion batteries primarily for Tesla Motors at the Tahoe Reno Industrial Centre in Storey County, Nevada, US, slated to be operational by 2015.

Dave Welmans

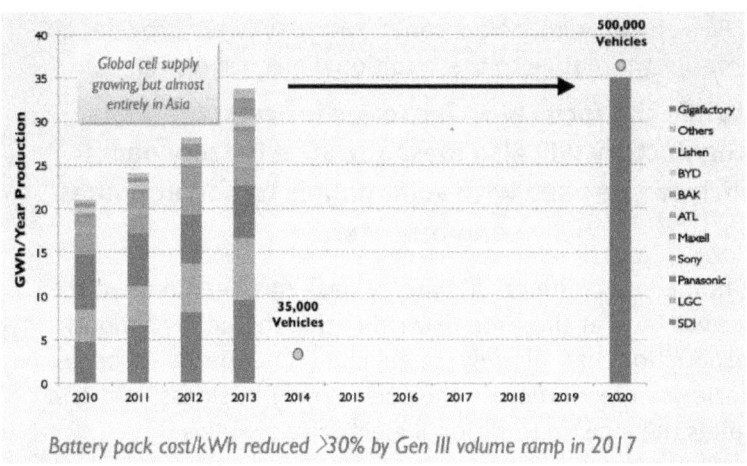

Battery pack cost/kWh reduced >30% by Gen III volume ramp in 2017

Musk is looking to focus on scaling the production of one of the most important and expensive parts of the electric car market and aims to achieve more than a 30% reduction in production costs for their car batteries when the new factory comes online. By 2020, this Gigafactory is projected to achieve a production capacity of 35 GWh/year of cells and 50 GWh/year of battery packs.

As the graphic shows, this is more than the rest of the current world production today. Other electronic companies that sell or rely on batteries are investing in the factory. Panasonic is said to have reached an agreement to invest in the factory.

The batteries will not only be for the Tesla and other electric cars but will also be producing batteries for other various uses such as drones, laptops, and grid energy storage.

In April 2015, Musk announced the home and business grid energy storage system, dubbed the Powerwall. By combining the Powerwall with solar panels, it may well provide an affordable alternative to the traditional electricity grid.

While the focus is on batteries for cars, the Tesla Gigafactory will also mass-produce battery packs which can be used with solar panels to power homes and business.

This home and commercial battery pack has been named the Powerwall and at the time of writing this the next 18 months of production has already been sold. Cheaper and better batteries can revolutionise the solar power business, and end people's reliance on traditional electricity supplies.

Concentrated solar power

Although the world has reached a grid-parity stage with conventional PV - where the cost of producing a watt of energy from PV is similar to the retail price of electricity in Africa – there are still substantial benefits to be garnered out of the technology.

I've already covered the drop in price for normal Photovoltaic (PV) systems but these standard systems can be improved. There are two main avenues to increase the performance of solar power. The first is using reflectors to concentrate the heat from the sun to drive a heat turbine. The second, and in my opinion more relevant to Africa, is low concentration PV. These are systems with a solar concentration of 2–100 suns, or brightness double to 100 times as bright as the sun. Conventional solar cells are typically used, and, at these concentrations, the cells do not need to be actively cooled. This simple addition can increase output 35% or more.

Dave Welmans

PV works on turning light energy into an electric current. The efficiency of this has a great impact on energy output. The relatively simple process of keeping the cells aligned optimally to the sun can increase efficiency by up to 50%. As described in the Digital Revolution chapter a simple computing device such as the Arduino with a light sensor and motors to align the cells will achieve this.

Together these two improvements can deliver almost double the electricity normally available from PV.

Batteries for Africa
As important as the production or harvesting of energy, is the ability to store this energy for use at appropriate times. Batteries are essential to any power revolution within Africa.

This supply of better and cheaper batteries is also aimed at home use and will prove to be a boon for Africa with its current energy challenges. The ability to operate efficiently in an inefficient energy environment will boost productivity and quality of life for Africans.

As discussed in the Energy chapter, alternative forms of energy production provide many opportunities within Africa. Underpinning these opportunities are the batteries for storage of this generated energy. Batteries may augment the traditional grid power as well as provide off-grid energy storage solutions throughout Africa. All Africans know the benefit of batteries, mostly due to the need for them in cellphones. Using battery technology together with solar or wind-generated energy is critical. With this adoption of battery technology, maybe one day Africa will also embrace the electric car for transport too.

Transport and drones

When a consumer-built and operated drone lands on the White House lawn, people tend to take notice. This is a technology that is already out there and is just waiting for people to make use of it to transform our world.

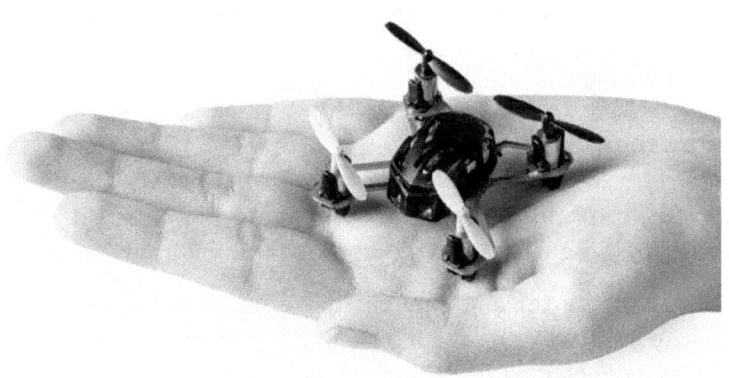

Drones or Unmanned Aerial Vehicles (UAVs) are simply a better version of remote-controlled and radio-controlled planes.

The growth in their use is due to a number of factors: cheaper and faster processors on the device while making use of something standard like an iPhone or Samsung phone or tablet as the controller has brought down the cost of making or buying one of these.

Drones can be large – to carry payloads, and small (nano-drones) - to be inconspicuous or cheap.

Beyond the military applications of UAVs with which "drones" have become most known, there are numerous civil

Dave Welmans

aviation uses. These uses include aerial surveying, taking aerial footage in filmmaking, wildlife management and conservation, use in disaster situations and even delivering supplies to remote or otherwise inaccessible regions.

The imagination knows no end to what can be augmented by a flying device with normally a camera on it: tourist reconnaissance operations, surveillance and security applications if accompanied by infrared capabilities, detection of poachers involved in illegal hunting and even crowd monitoring at public venues and events.

Its easy to see why drones are desperately needed in Africa - to help with activities like aerial surveillance to monitoring of borders as well as coastlines to monitor and identify illegal fishing vessels and in national parks and in national parks to help conserve the threatened African fauna.

Flying donkeys?

One of the basic needs in Africa is moving goods across its at worst dangerous and perilous road networks, but at best difficult and remote. As more and more Africans become connected in the virtual world, the demand for goods that are being bought or sold will escalate. A far-thinking Kenyan organisation has dubbed the Flying Donkey, which is a cargo drone that is commercialised and has industrial quality components with rugged airframes and lifting capabilities better than current models. This organisation has set up a challenge to stimulate interest and investment in this particular space. They plan to have the first commercial flying donkey flying in Africa by 2020. The success criteria are the ability to carry at least 20kg over 50km in less than one hour.

Taking from road networks, the organisation recommends creating air corridors for these flying donkeys. The aim is to help grow the transport and logistics industry particular to Africa and thereby help create jobs and stimulate economic growth.

The Flying Donkey Challenge is organised and funded by Swiss non-profit organisation, La Fondation Bundi. Their goal is to develop a class of donkey that can be used to carry goods to market and deliver medication to remote villages amongst other duties. The idea has gained international interest with 33 teams from around the world entering the competition.

A Kenyan engineer James Munyoki has built several drones. He has made significant progress and his latest prototype can carry 6 kilograms. He is almost half way to the 5-year goal of the 20kg payload.

Google, as usual, is also at the forefront of investigating this technology. They are in the initial phase of development of their project in this space – called Project Wing. The Google design is unique in that it uses an unusual design called a tail sitter. This tail sitter is a hybrid of a plane and a helicopter that can take off vertically, like a military vertical take off and landing (VTOL) which then rotates to a horizontal position for flying around. They have also adopted a winch dropping system for delivery of packages. They attach electronic sensors to the package called the "egg". This detects when the package has been deposited and then retracts back into the drone for the return journey.

Dave Welmans

As with the telecoms network in the sky covered earlier, having Google invest in this technology helps give impetus to the whole industry helping catalyse all the efforts mentioned here home hobbyist efforts to Ledgard's different flying donkey vision.

3-D printing

3-D printing sounds like the stuff of science fiction: a technology that potentially can create any object of one's imagination, even human organs, with just a few computer instructions.

A 3-D printer uses computer images to make — or "print" — three-dimensional objects. 3-D printers can be used to create anything from plastic toys and jewellery to a prosthetic limb and even a gun.

3-D printing has been around since 1983 when Charles Hull invented stereo lithography: a process that builds objects one layer at a time. 3-D printing technology was originally used to rapidly develop prototypes, hard-to-find parts and unique designs. The speed of being able to create a workable physical model cost-effectively and relatively quickly can transform business by allowing companies to design and print their own prototypes and models. This obviates the need to send the job out to another manufacturing company.

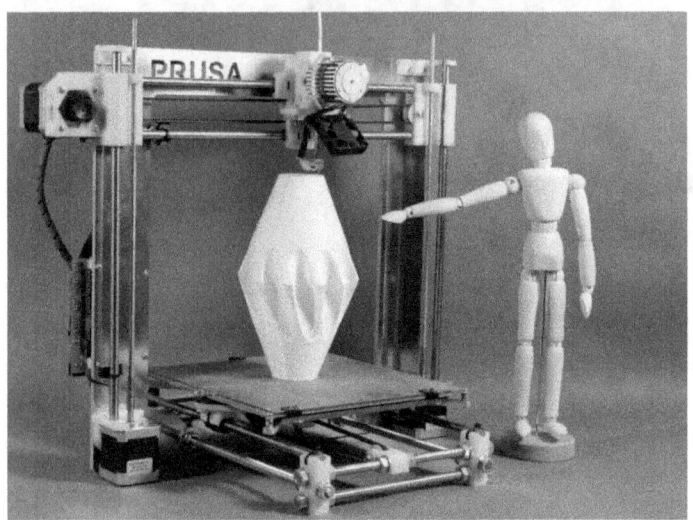

FDM/SLS/DLP
Three major forms of 3-D printing exist today

- – FDM (Fused Deposition Modelling).
- – DLP (Digital Light Projection).
- – SLS (Selective Laser Sintering).

FDM melts a substance – usually a plastic – and acts as an intelligent glue gun. DLP uses light to cure a resin while SLS sinters or 'welds' a powder being deposited with laser technology.

The technology is already used extensively in jewellery design, dentistry, manufacturing and design, architecture, engineering, construction, automotive and aerospace.

Dave Welmans

The last 10 years has seen the advent of the home 3-D printer. They are cheaper and less sophisticated than the industrial printers. We are one step closer to the Star Trek world of printing anything on demand. The Internet Café of Africa might become the 3-D printing shop of Africa.

Obama said in 2014 that 3-D printing has "the potential to revolutionise the way we make almost everything."

As with expensive paper printers previously, everybody does do not need to own a 3-D printer but can follow the bureau model of using a centralised printing service that specialises in high quality printing to take advantage of this technology.

So where does that leave 3-D printing in Africa? It is still at this stage a revolutionary technology best suited for unique products for both consumer and business uses, but the process is not yet efficient enough for mass production.

Africa more often needs specific parts than production, which means that 3-D printing is almost custom-made for Africa.

The cost of low-end 3-D printers has fallen to the extent that there is now a $60 DLP resin printer on the Instructables website together with the recipe to make light sensitive resin for the printer. This means that almost anybody can build his or her own 3-D printer. Africa needs to take advantage of this disruptive technology for itself.

RepRap
The RepRap is the invention of Adrian Boywer, a professor of engineering at Bath University. He developed a cheap open-source hardware and software version and allowed the open-

source community to share and develop the project. This was enthusiastically adopted by the world and cheaper variations are making it into the hobbyist community.

3-D printing in Togo

Togo is a small African country next to Ghana on the West coast of Africa and has only 6 million inhabitants while being about 40% the size of England. This former French colony is

also one of the poorest nations in Africa coming in just ahead of Zimbabwe and the DRC so you might be surprised to find a fully-fledged maker space here.

A maker space is a workshop environment where inventors and tinkerers can work on new projects within this community. Woelab bills itself as *"Africa's first space for democratic technology"*. One of the sudents there, Afate's recently unveiled his 3-D printer made from discarded computer parts. The recycled computer parts used to make the printer are they type of electronics that can be found in any electronics dump.

The innovation of the 3-D printer is one thing, but when Afate combined this with an African crowdsourcing platform, Ulule, he came up with magic. Ulule raised $4000 to further develop a 3-D printer and Afate built his prototype 3-D printer using less than $100 in parts.

Following this success, Afate is now working on setting up a chain of 3D printing hubs specific for Africa. This will

Dave Welmans

integrate into cyber café's and give access to many more communities to understand and learn about 3-D printing while at the same time democratising the manufacturing of the printer from recycled parts.

"My dream is to give young people hope and to show that Africa, too, has its place on the global market when it comes to technology. We are able to create things. Why is Africa always lagging behind when it comes to technology?" the inventor asked.

Afate's 3-D printer is a replica of the Adrian Boywer open-source 3-D model. The main contribution that Afate has made is to show how this technology can be manufactured from already available old computer parts and to spread his passion and knowledge in true African fashion.

FabLab

FabLabs are a concept that originated as the educational outreach component of Massachusetts Institute of Technology's (MIT) funded Centre  for Bits & Atoms (CBA). This is similar to maker space projects and they have a small but professional setup with industrial grade tools and computers. They follow the open-source methodology.

These FabLabs are smaller versions of a production factory. Their aim is not to run production but rather to give people access to the tools necessary to design and test products. This is ideal for people looking to create prototypes for all types of industries from architecture to engineering. The added availability of computers with open-source design software becomes the prologue to send to cutting and milling machines.

The Fablab helps create a minfset of 'can do' attitude aimed at the youth and can go a long ay to helping bridge the digital divide in underprivileged areas. As mentioned in the education chapter, this community of equipment, knowledge and mentors help young entrepreneurs overcome the barriers to realising their designs and dreams.

Who could imagine a better learning centre for Africa?

3-D printing In South Africa
The major South African investment in 3-D printing has been in the additive manufacturing of titanium.

The Titanium Centre of Competence, with a price tag of about R200m ($20m), is an umbrella organisation that co-ordinates the country's technological development, with the aim of developing and commercialising South Africa's titanium industry.

Titanium has many uses in manufacturing for many sectors including aerospace and aviation. The metal is also extensively in the medical field for inserts and prosthesis, e.g. hip joints. The National Laser Centre at the Council for Scientific and Industrial Research (CSIR) has collaborated with the South African aerospace manufacturer Aerosud on a $4m project to further develop additive manufacturing products and techniques.

Aerosud is already a major component supplier to Airbus and Boeing, producing almost a million parts a year.

Dave Welmans

"South Africa is the second-largest supplier of titanium mineral ore, but adds little value to that before export,"

Derek Hanekom, the deputy minister of science and technology, said at the launch of the project in 2012.

These two companies have developed a specialised laser to be used to build parts directly for these industries. The current prototype uses the titanium metal powder and is already more than 8 times faster than traditional systems.

But 3-D printing doesn't stop there. There are still a myriad of ways in which 3-D prototyping and manufacturing can be used to benefit society. Anything from a new hand to a house, you can 3-D-print almost anything.

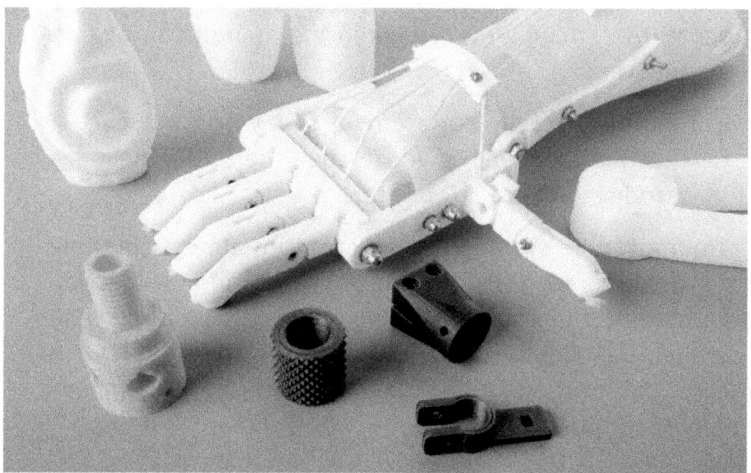

Source - http://www.3-Diot.net/

Enter Robohand. Richard van As lost four fingers in a woodworking accident 15 years ago and Richard then used 3-D printing technology to print himself a new hand, which he dubbed "Robohand". Following his passion, Richard designed his own 3-D printer, the Robobeast, and following his passion started printing prosthetics for people focussing on kids. Traditional prosthetics are extremely expensive and time-consuming to manufacture and it is a field that lends itself well to this technology. Children are particularly good as a target market as they fast growth means that they need to adjust the size of their prosthetics on a regular basis. Most families cannot afford a single prosthetic, never mind having to invest in a new one every six months or so. Richard's Robobeast helps these people.

Google followed suite with this initiative and partially funded e-NABLE, an organisation that specialises in printing prosthetics for children. They made an award of $600 000 to help this worthy organisation.

This is already changing everything in the manufacturing and engineering sector.

3-D printing has literally gone out of this world. A Space-X Dragon capsule touched down at the International Space Station, carrying with it a 3-D printer.

3-D printing can be scaled up in size to print almost anything and there seems to be a race on in the home construction field with numerous companies vying to be the first and then the fastest 3-D house printing companies. First, a Dutch company 3-D-printed a house followed by a Chinese company that managed to 10 houses in less than 24 hours.

Dave Welmans

ISS commander Barry 'Butch' Wilmore with the finished socket wrench. Photograph: Nasa

"3-D printing serves as a fast and inexpensive way to manufacture parts on site and on demand, reducing the need for costly spares on the International Space Station and future spacecraft," the US National Aeronautics & Space Administration said.

The applications are obviously endless and what is helping drive this technology revolution at such a rapid rate is that most of the technology has been made open-source. WikiHouse is another house printing organisation. Their aim is to make the technology as widely available as possible so that anyone can download and print the necessary components for homes.

The benefit of being able to cheaply and quickly prototype parts will be a major boon for Africans, who have been excluded from innovation due to the high cost of participation.

The Last Billion

The ability to produce a part that is not easily available sounds like everyone in Africa will need access to 3-D printers to solve this particularly African dilemma.

Open-sourcing industry

Finally, for this chapter, I'd like to focus on the disruptive nature of the open-source methodology and its impact on grass-roots industry - the heart of a free market system. The production or harvesting, transport, sale and consumption are the basis of our economies.

Africa has been left behind when it comes to industry due to a myriad of factors, some of which I've touched on in the introductory chapters of this book. Africans need access to technology and the knowledge needed in order to apply basic skills that can change their lives at, literally, a grass-roots level.

One particular initiative by a small group of dedicated people may help change this. The Open-Source Ecology (OSE)

Dave Welmans

organisation has as its aim to establish an open-source economy that "...is an efficient economy which increases innovation by open collaboration." In order to do this the founder, Marcin Jakubowski, has defined and continues to develop with input from the rest of the world, the Global Village Construction Set (GVSC). This construction set is made up of 50 of the most important machines that it takes for modern life to exist – everything from a tractor, to an oven, to a circuit maker.

A Princeton University and University of Wisconsin graduate in fusion physics, Jakubowksi and his team are producing open-source blueprints to help people create, build and maintain everyday machines at a cost much lower than required in a proprietary environment. His goal is to create the equivalent of a large-scale LEGO set of powerful, self-replicating production tools. Their stated aim is to help these products to be manufactured in a decentralised, royalty free manner in order to achieve self-sustainable modern societies that rely on their local economies.

If anyone had to develop a blueprint for unleashing individual potential in Africa, this would be it!

Despite the altruistic aim of the organisation, it is rooted in practical delivery of the basic technology people need to survive. It is intended to be a kernel for building infrastructures of modern civilisation.

The goal of the organisation is to make it easier for remote villages in Third World countries as well as small enterprises to have access to the relevant tools to help them create better lives for themselves.

The definition of the end outcome of this construction set is to allow 12 people working for a together in a community with less than two hours per day and relying solely on local resources to be able to sustain themselves and their families while helping them take part in the modern world economy.

The backbone of Open-Source Ecology is open access to economically significant information – product designs, techniques, and rapid learning materials for achieving this. This collaborative development with information on the best practices used is made available via the Internet.

When economic productivity is unleashed as such, there is a direct effect on community prosperity. As a result of lowered barriers to entry, each community can increase the range of products and services that it can provide.

This is an impressive approach to social upliftment for communities and has attracted support and awards from many organisations including the Shuttleworth Foundation.

Another example of the open-source community and its possible impact on Africa comes from OpenKnit. OpenKnit is an open-source, low-cost, digital fabrication tool that affords the user the opportunity to create his own bespoke clothing from digital files. This is equivalent to designs for a 3-D printer, but instead of filament and Gcode, it uses yarn and designs being shared are fabric designs and patterns. This leverages off the best of the Internet community by helping people go directly from the raw material and straight to its final product. Tis could be a sweater or a dress. This open-source project relies on other open-source developed hardware, in this case, the famous Arduino mentioned in The Digital Revolution chapter.

Summary: Future Technological Disruptors

- Telecoms connectivity may be disrupted by high-altitude balloons; or
- Low Earth Orbit Satellites; and
- Unmanned perpetual drones;
- Transport may be disrupted by the introduction of drones and '"Flying Donkeys" in Africa;
- 3-D printing is perfectly suited to solve Africa's problems of availability and distance; and
- Open-source methodology of development across industries can benefit Africa hugely.

Dave Welmans

15.Epilogue

Africa has long been viewed as "the hopeless continent" by the outside world and often for many very good reasons. Wars, hunger and famine, lack of infrastructure, despots and corruption all contribute to this "hopeless" perception.

The aim of this book was to present a realistic view on the current state of the continent across a wide range of industries and note the effect that technology is having in these different sectors.

The overriding outlook is a positive and improving one with multiple reasons for this, most notably the increased economic stability and governance, often brought about by a positive outside influence.

The last 15 years have shown that Africa can be independent, self-sustaining and can follow the route of globalisation to be meaningfully incorporated into the world economy.

The single largest factor, in my view, for this improvement, is the introduction of improved communication, in the form of cellular communication, which has put Africa within reach of the rest of the world.

Although it is the cellular and digital revolution that have had a great impact on Africans, it is the coming broadband revolution, based on this original technological framework that has the potential of having an even greater beneficial effect.

I have attempted to make clear that technology itself is not the only requirement for this revolution, but rather an African-specific strategy, that takes into account particular

African conditions and challenges, will be needed to overcome the many obstacles on this path to prosperity.

Energy production is a constraint on African growth, but alternative energy solutions may allow Africa to bypass the First World fossil fuel trap and benefit the world as a whole.

The ability for Africa to make use of the technology available today, and those technologies on the horizon, delivering Africa-specific solutions, coupled with Africa's ability to capitalise on these, will largely dictate the success of the next decades for the continent.

Facts about Africa

Search for #theafricathemedianevershowsyou on Twitter for an uplifting view of Africa.

Countries in Africa sorted by population:

Nigeria	184 264 000
Ethiopia	90 076 000
Egypt	88 523 000
Democratic Rep. Congo	71 246 000
South Africa	54 844 000
Tanzania	48 829 000
Kenya	44 090 000
Algeria	39 903 000
Sudan	38 435 000
Uganda	35 760 000
Morocco	33 680 000
Ghana	27 714 000
Mozambique	25 728 000
Angola	25 326 000
Ivory Coast	23 326 000

Dave Welmans

Madagascar	23 053 000
Cameroon	21 918 000
Niger	18 880 000
Burkina Faso	18 450 000
Mali	17 796 000
Malawi	16 307 000
Zambia	15 474 000
Senegal	14 150 000
Chad	13 675 000
Zimbabwe	13 503 000
South Sudan	12 519 000
Rwanda	11 324 000
Tunisia	11 118 000
Somalia	10 972 000
Guinea	10 935 000
Benin	10 750 000
Burundi	9 824 000
Togo	7 065 000
Eritrea	6 895 000
Libya	6 521 000
Sierra Leone	6 513 000
Central African Rep.	5 545 000
Republic of the Congo	4 706 000
Liberia	4 046 000
Mauritania	3 632 000
Gabon	2 382 000
Namibia	2 281 000
Botswana	2 176 000
Gambia	2 022 000
Equatorial Guinea	1 996 000
Lesotho	1 908 000
Guinea-Bissau	1 788 000
Mauritius	1 263 000

Swaziland	1 119 000
Djibouti	961 000
Comoros	783 000
Cape Verde	525 000
São Tomé and Príncipe	194 000
Seychelles	97 000

Dave Welmans

ABOUT THE AUTHOR

Dave Welmans was born in a small gold mining town in South Africa and graduated from the University of Witwatersrand. He has travelled extensively in Africa for both business and pleasure over the last 30 years.

He has climbed Kilimanjaro in Tanzania, Africa's highest peak at 5895m/19,341ft. Dave still loves jumping on a plane and disappearing into Africa for relaxation.

He is an experienced telecoms professional, having worked in this field for more than a decade. His deep-rooted African-ness colours his passion for all things African and with his 25 years experience in ICT and telecoms combine to provide the input into The Last Billion.

Dave lives and works in Johannesburg, doing business consulting and running a 3-D printing company. He does public speaking on technology and Africa.

www.ingramcontent.com/pod-product-compliance
Lightning Source LLC
Chambersburg PA
CBHW051903170526
45168CB00001B/221